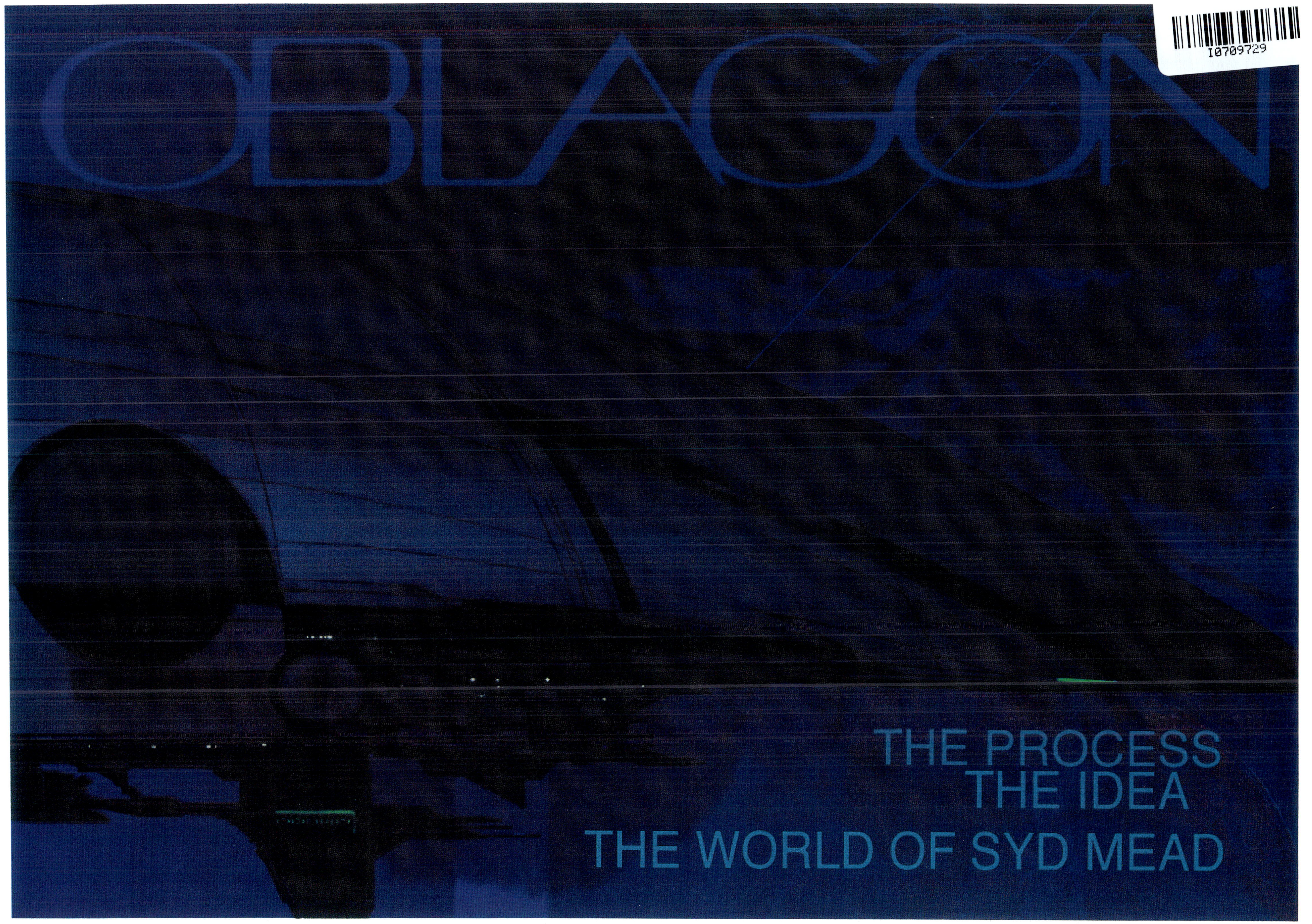
OBLAGON
THE PROCESS
THE IDEA
THE WORLD OF SYD MEAD

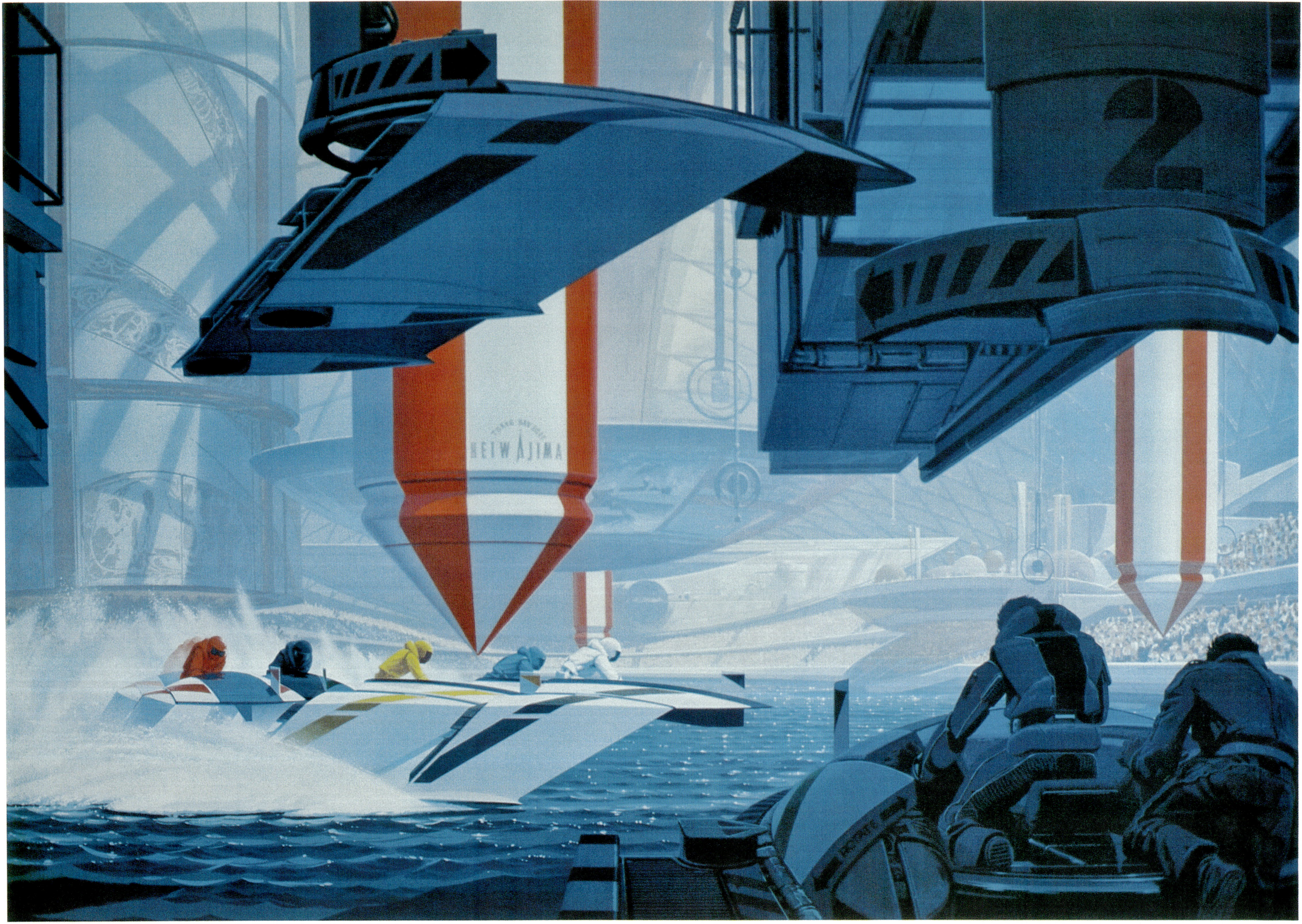

2
HEIWAJIMA
2

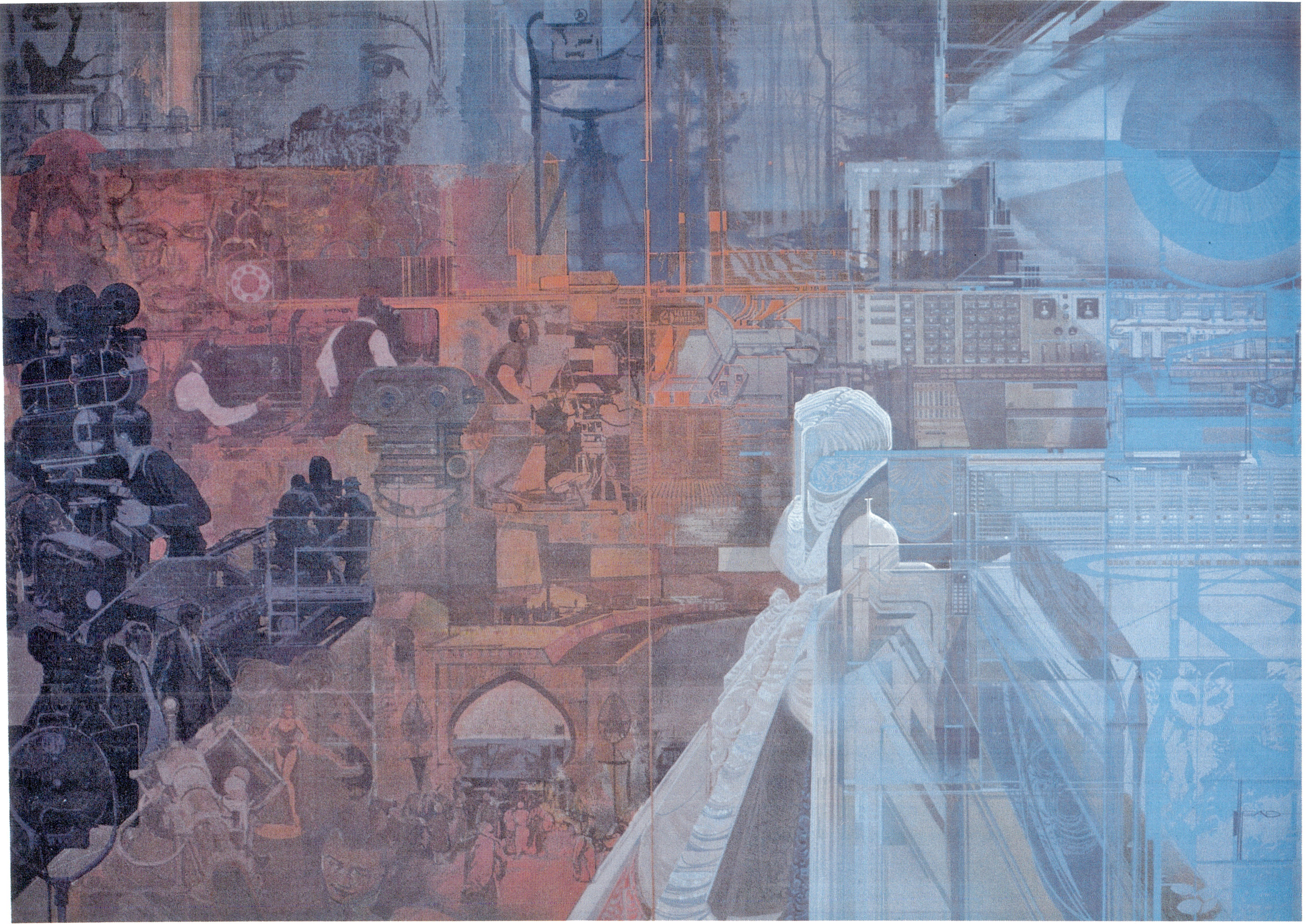

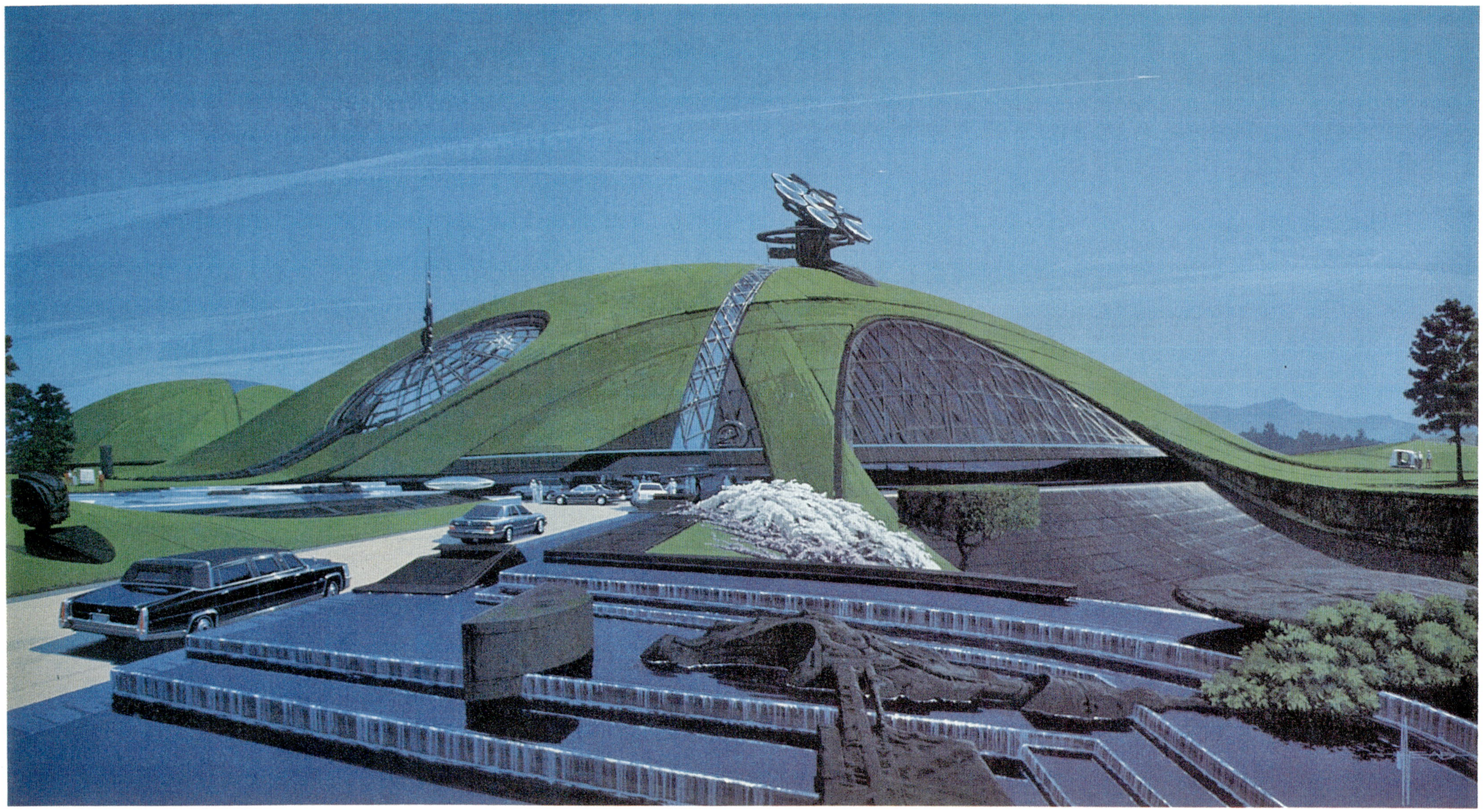

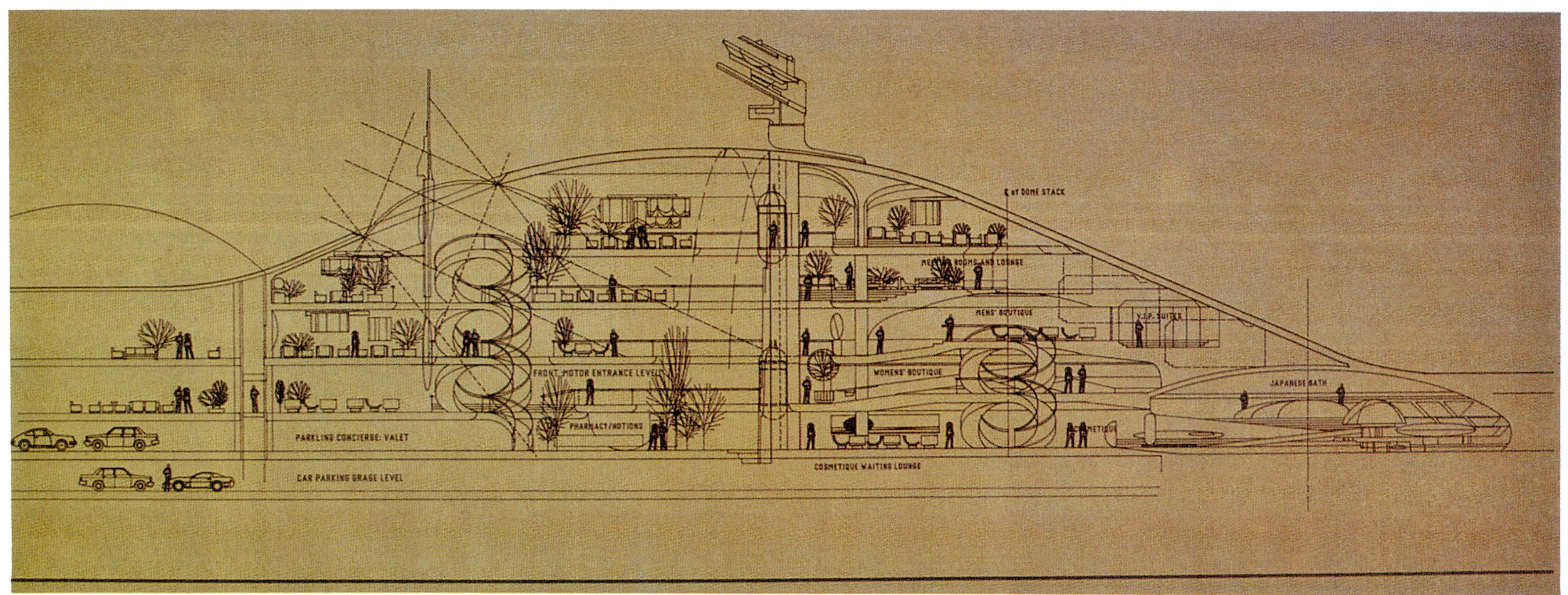
C at DOME STACK
MEETING ROOMS AND LOUNGE
MENS' BOUTIQUE
V.I.P. SUITES
WOMENS' BOUTIQUE
JAPANESE BATH
COSMETIQUE
FRONT MOTOR ENTRANCE LEVEL
PHARMACT/NOTIONS
PARKLING CONCIERGE: VALET
COSMETIQUE WAITING LOUNGE
CAR PARKING GRAGE LEVEL

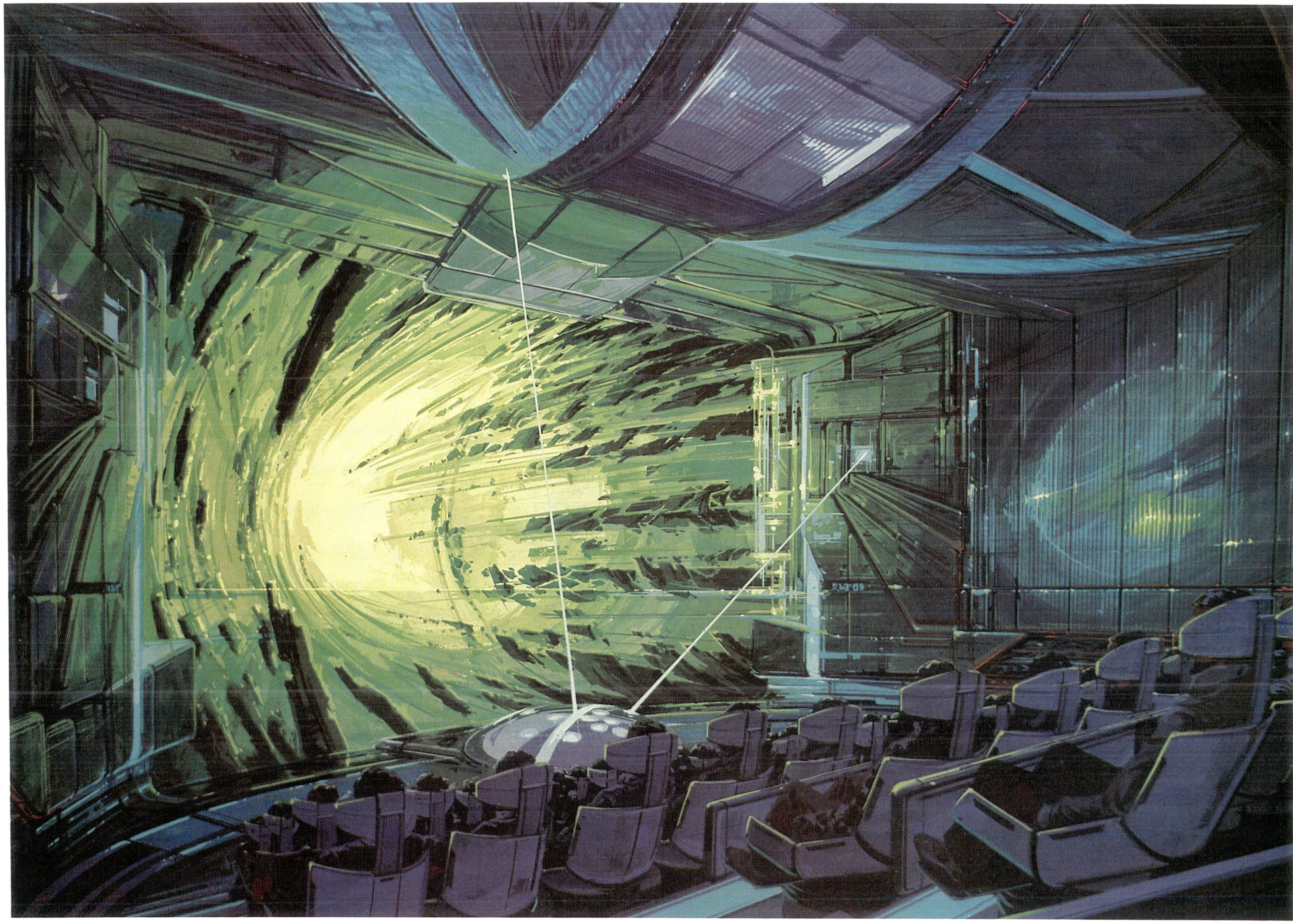

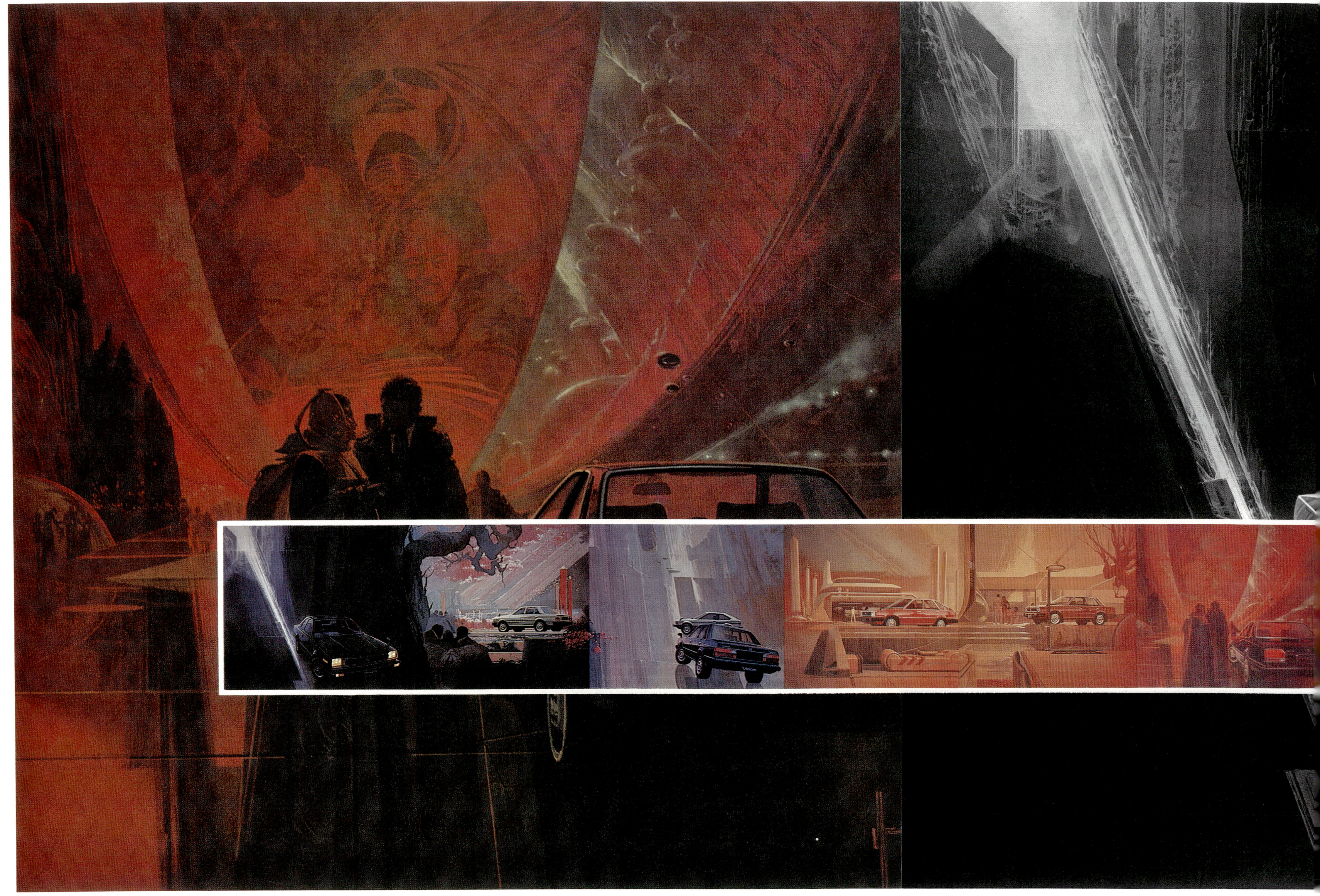

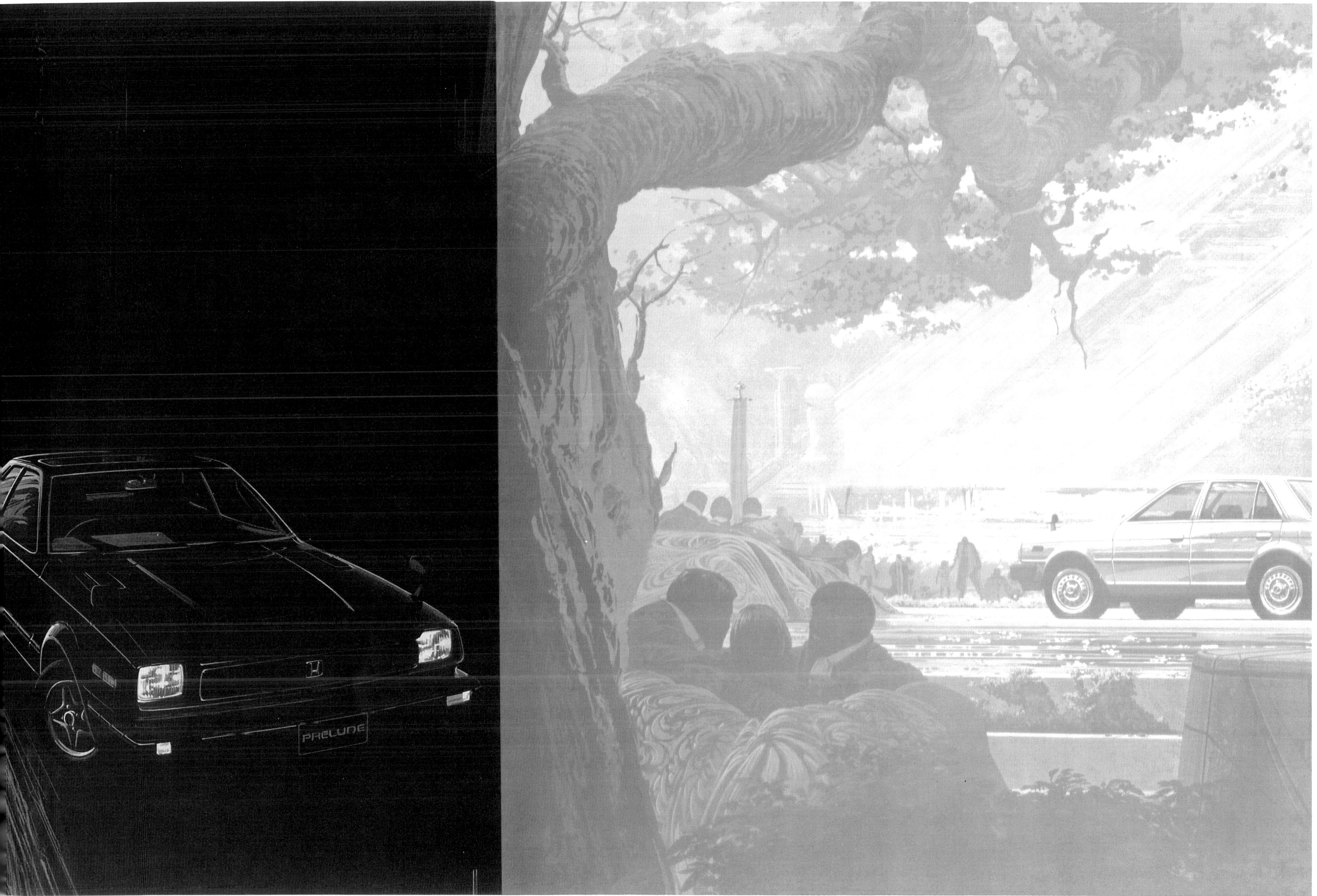

PRELUDE
honda

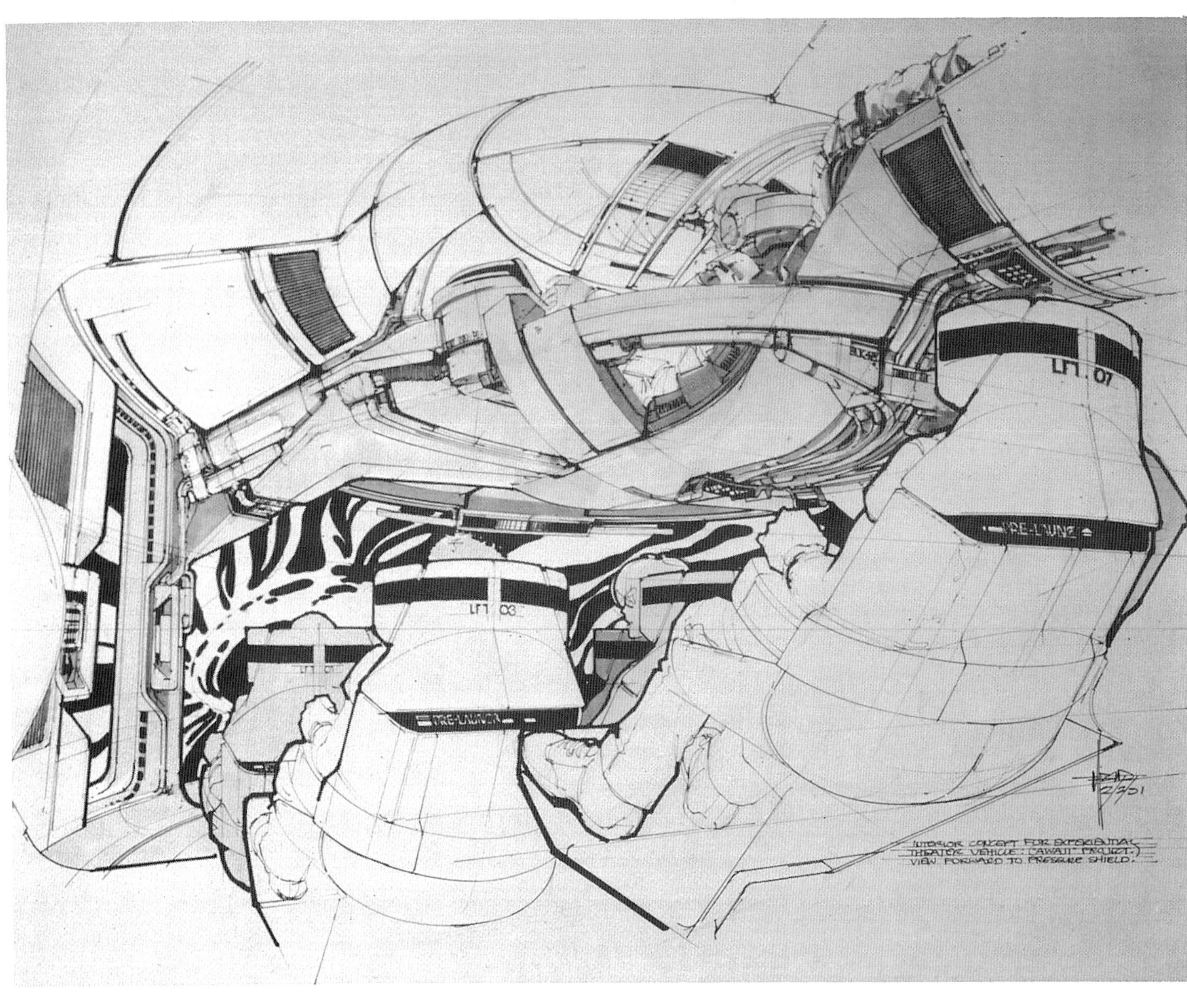

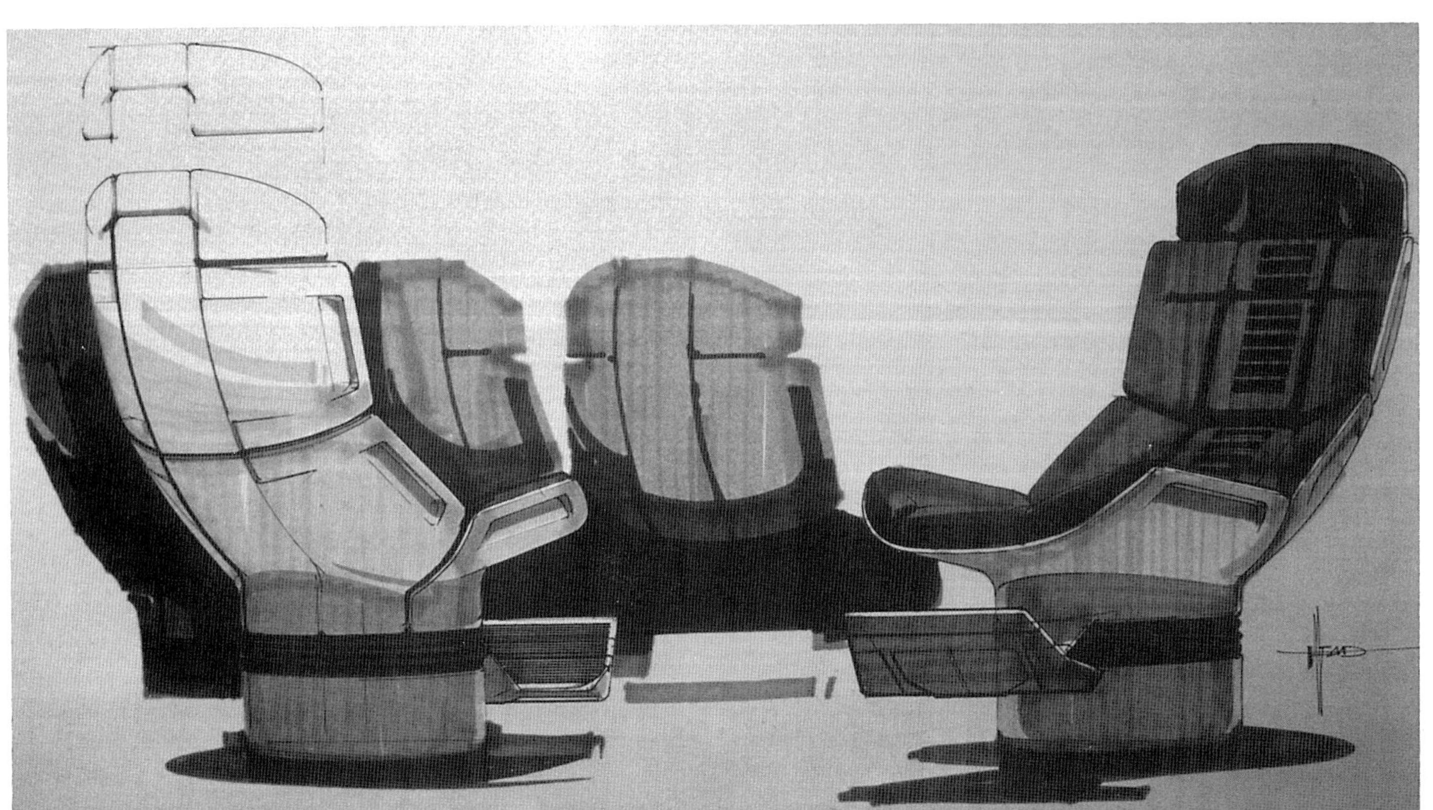

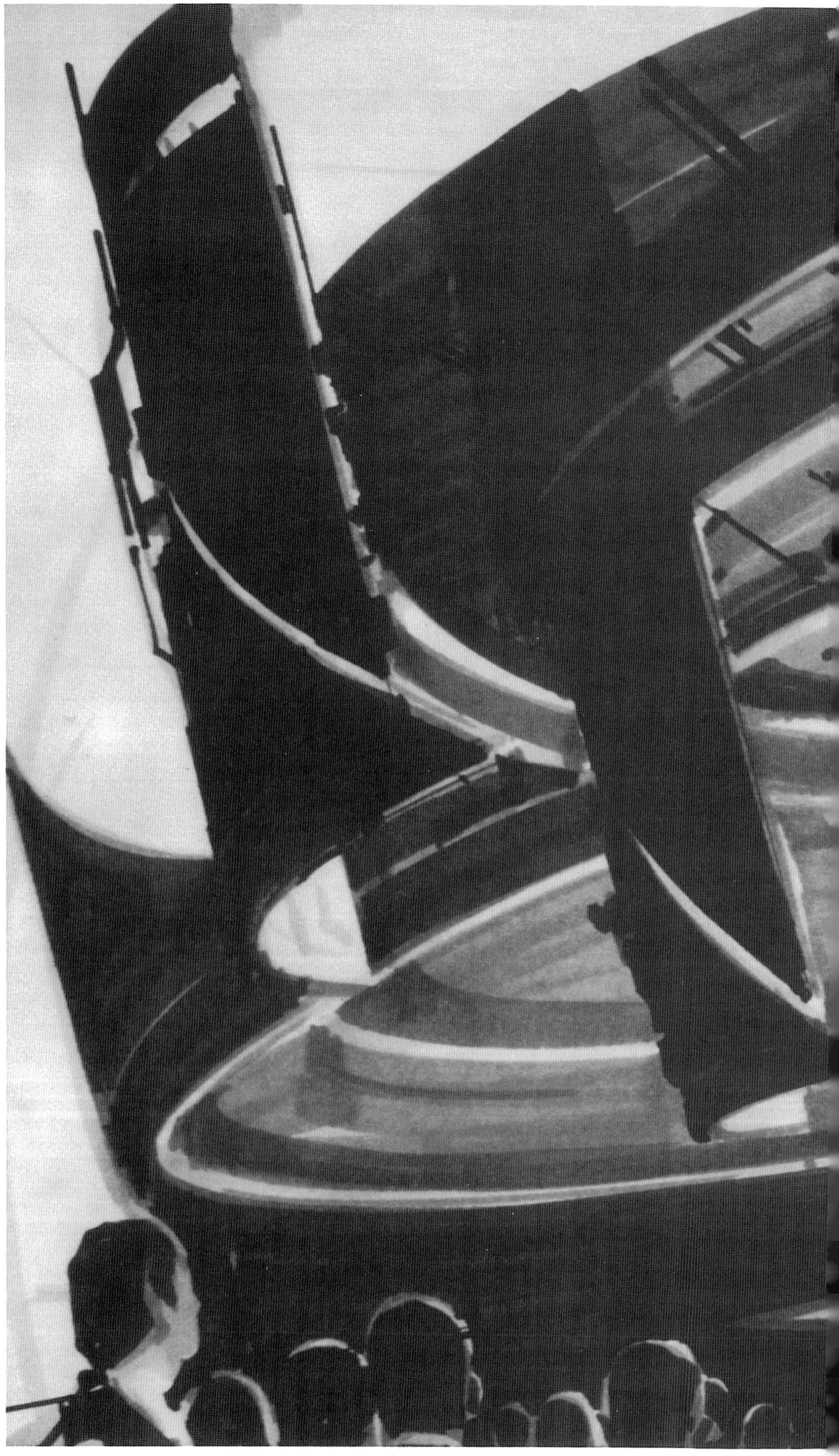

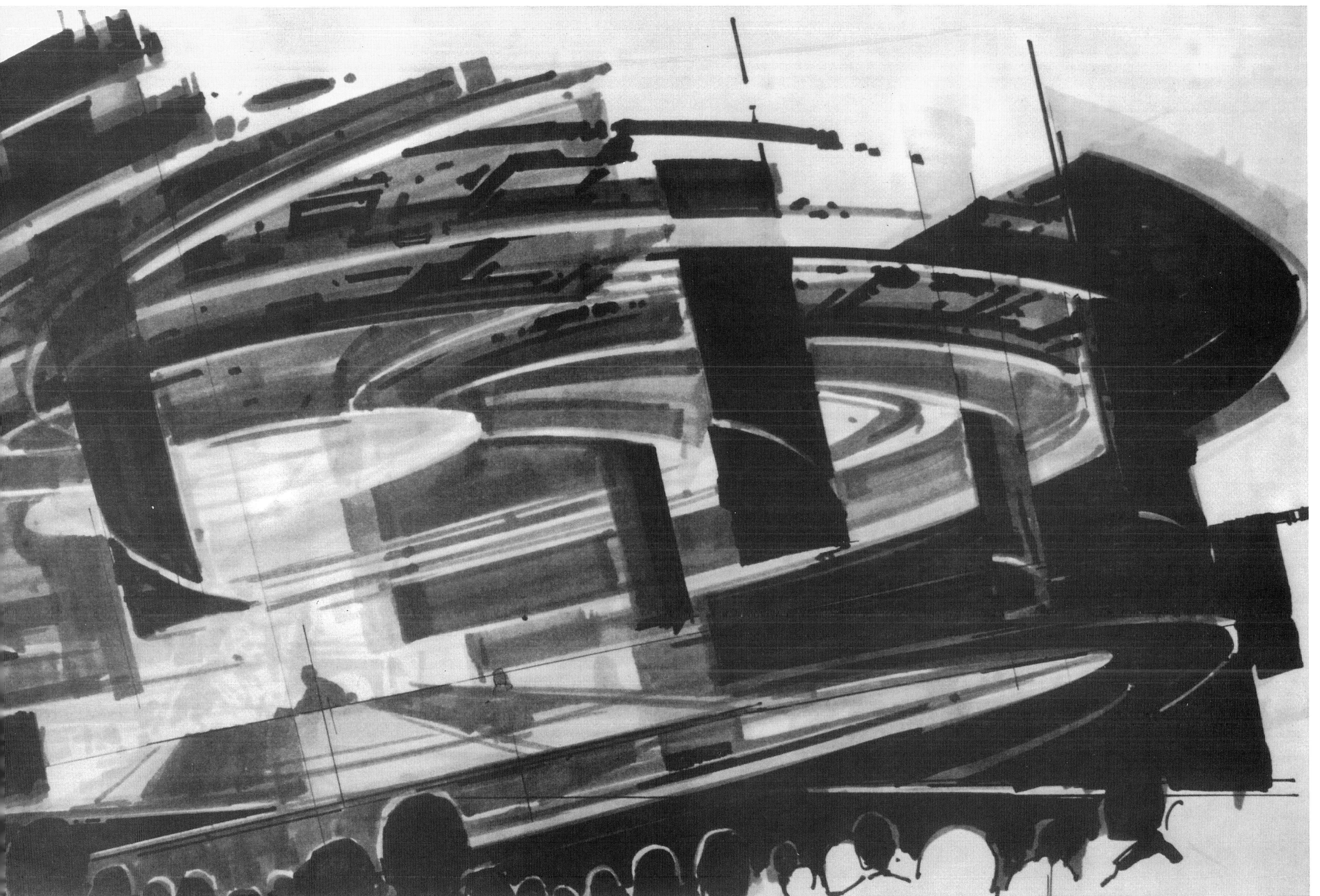

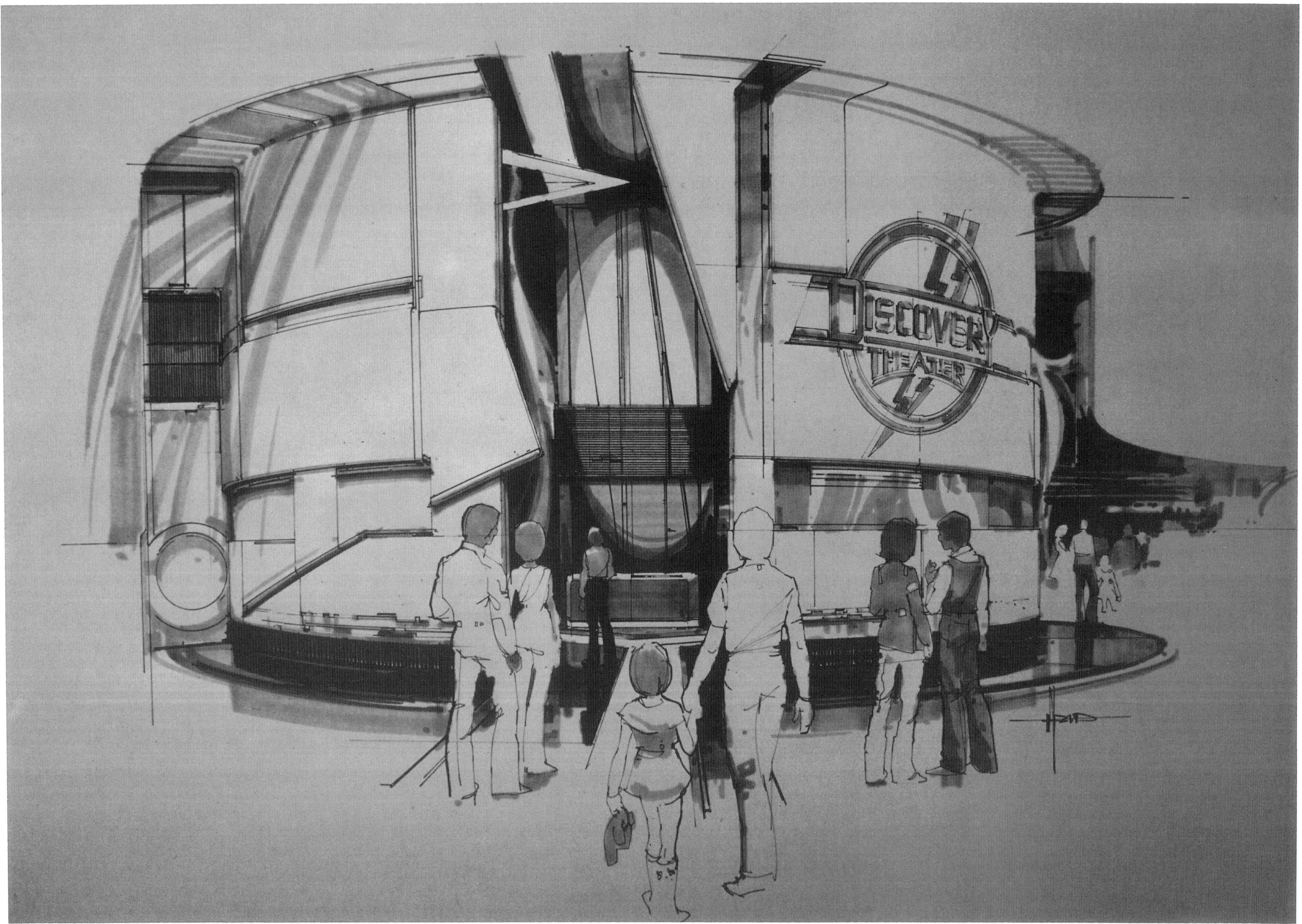

DISCOVERY
THEATER

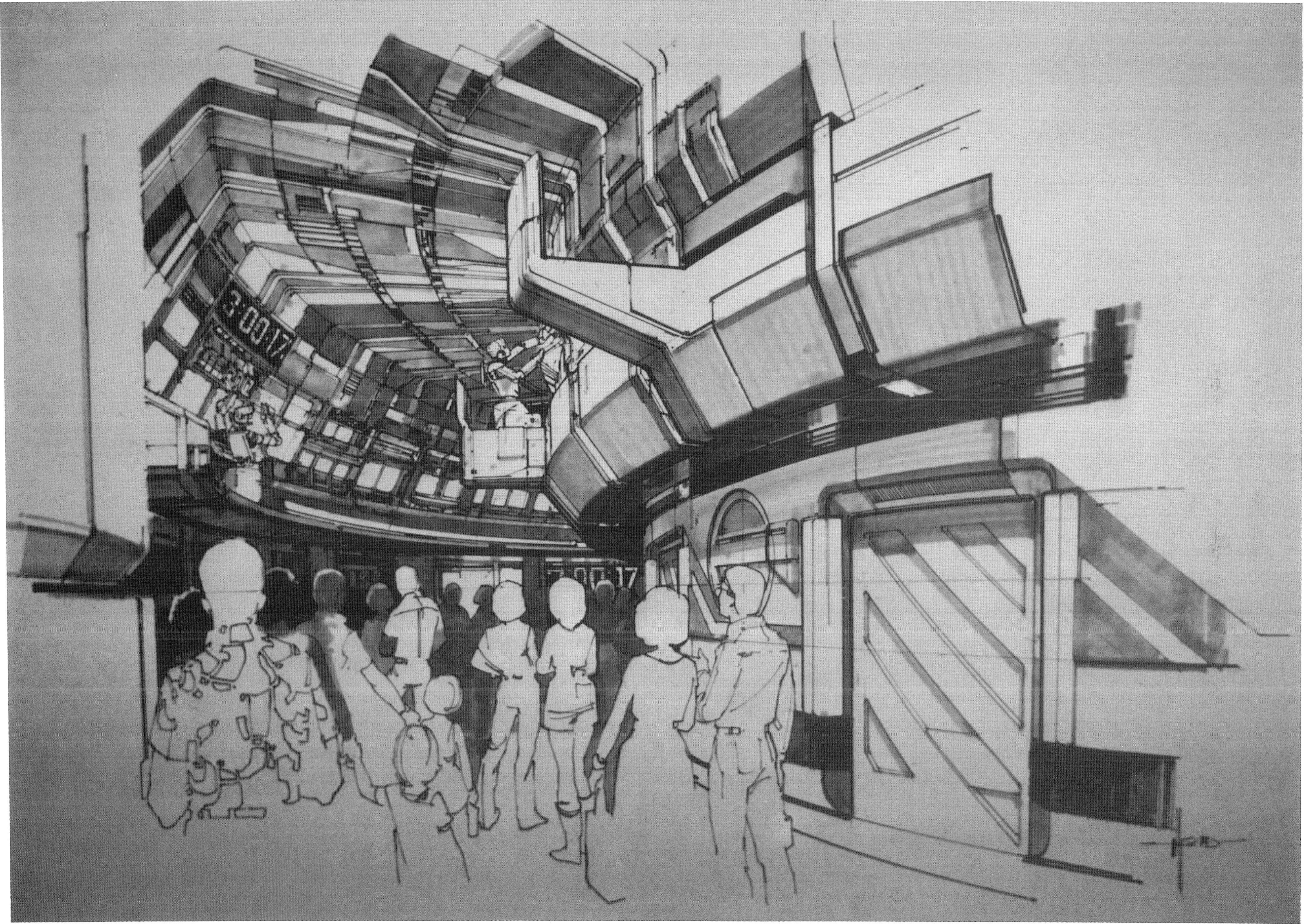3:00:17
7:00:17

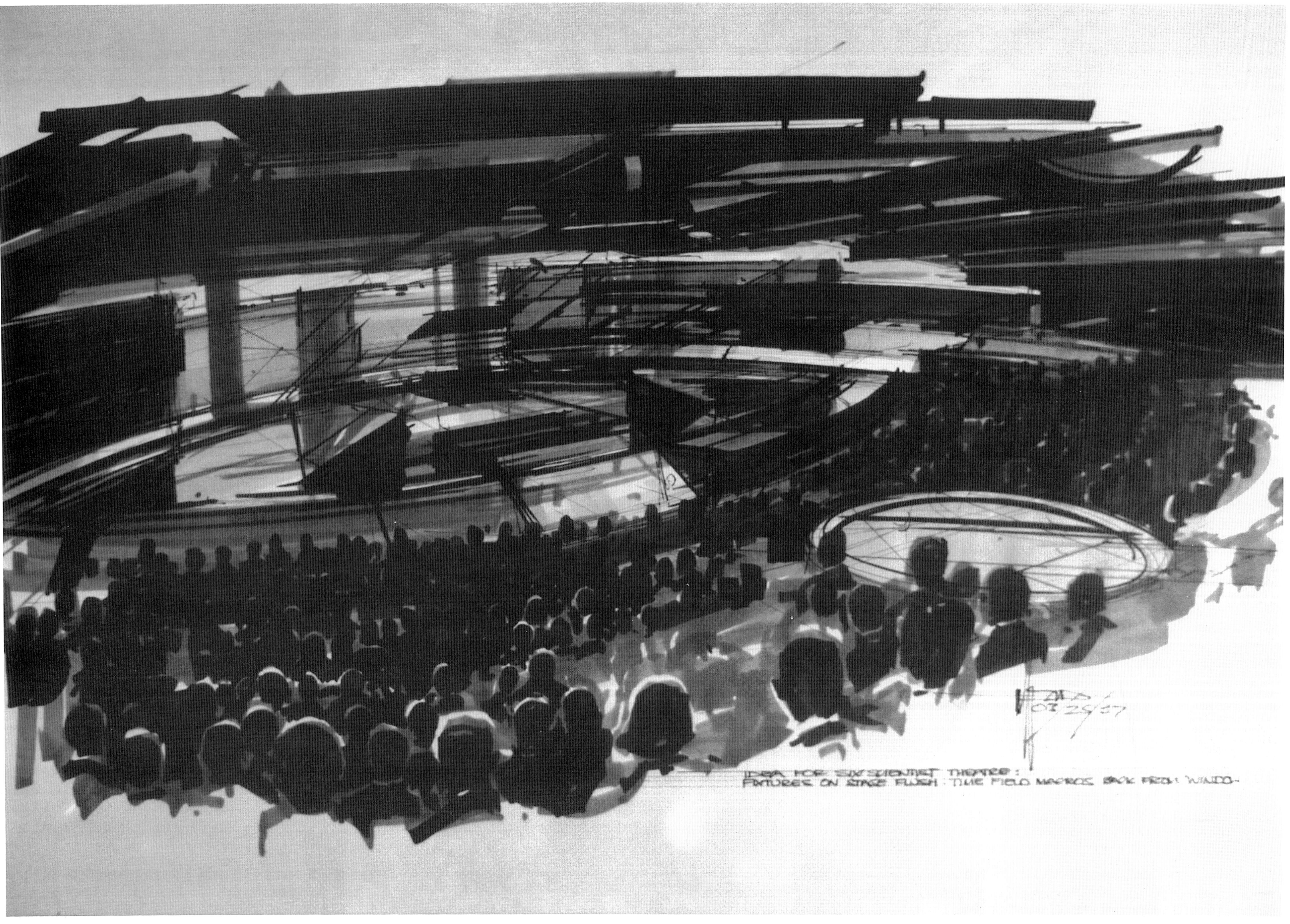

IDEA FOR SIX SCIENTIST THEATRE:
FIXTURES ON STAGE FLUSH. TIME FIELD MACROS BACK FROM WINDO-

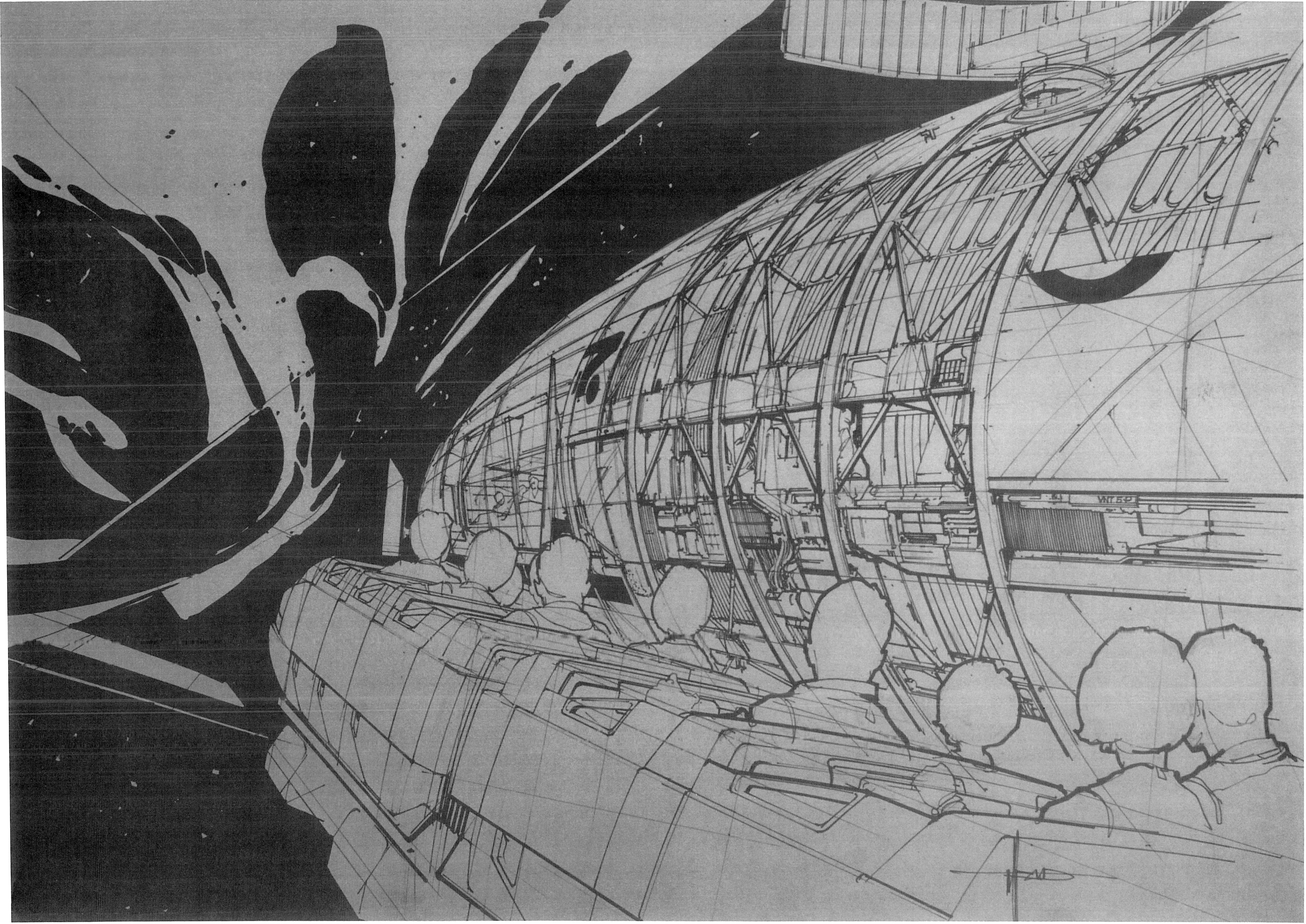

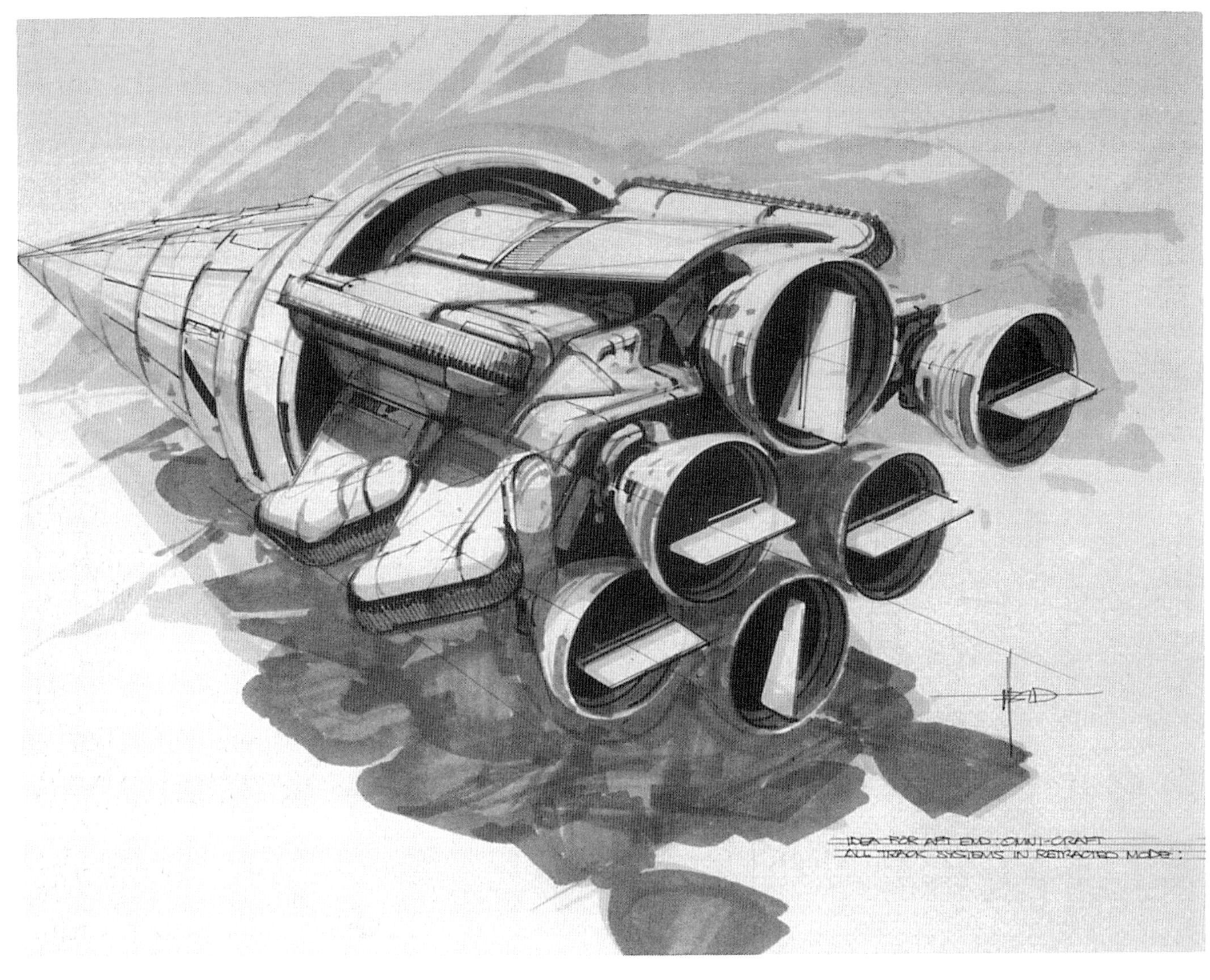
IDEA FOR AFT END SHUTTLE-CRAFT.
ALL TRACK SYSTEMS IN RETRACTED MODE.

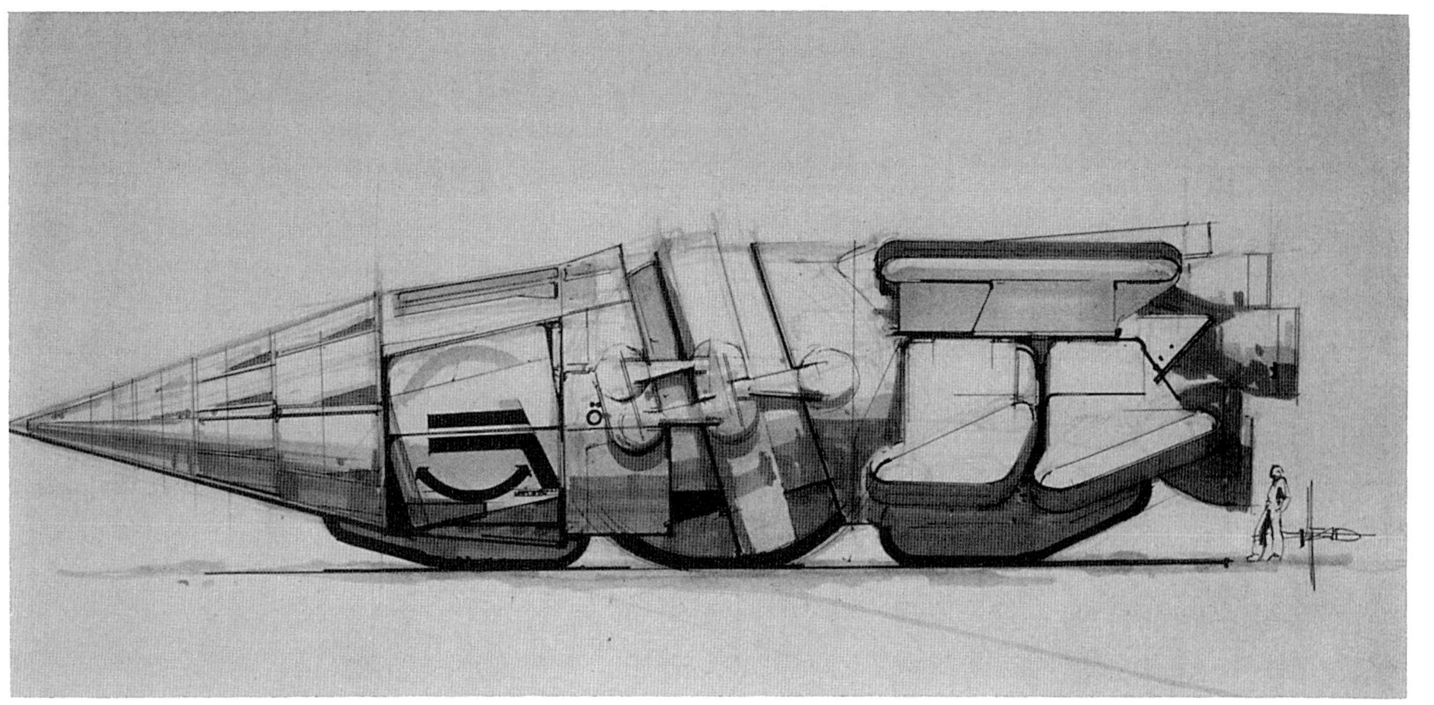

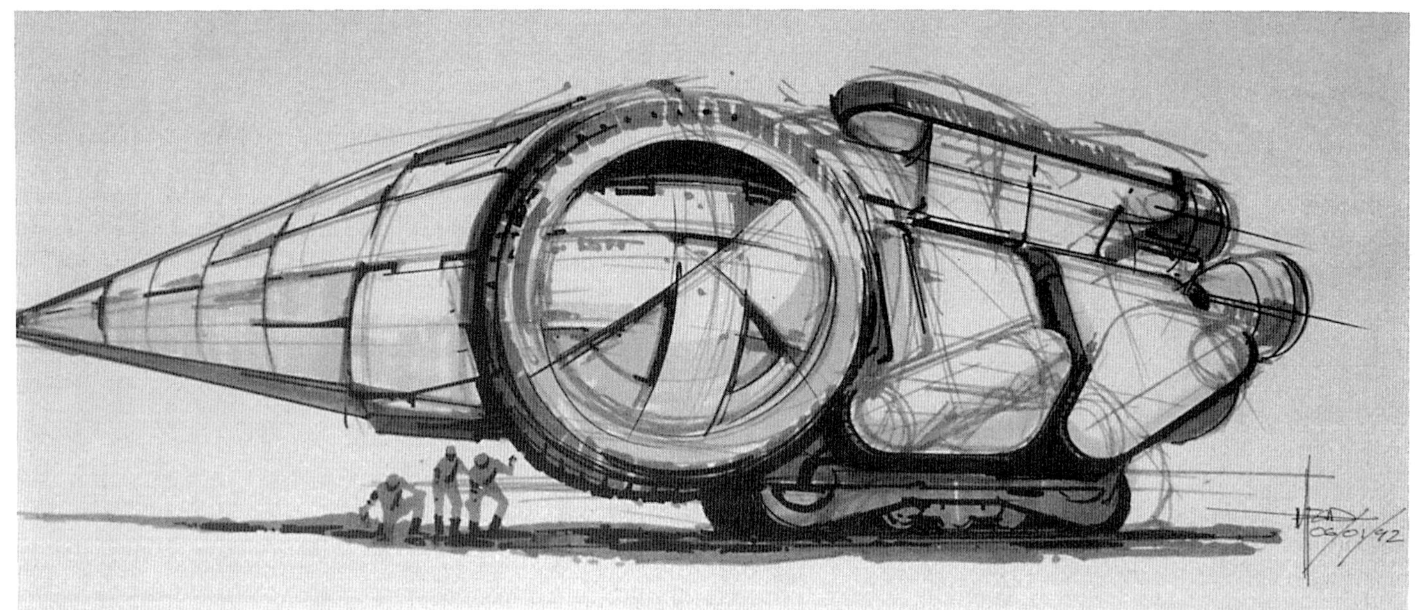

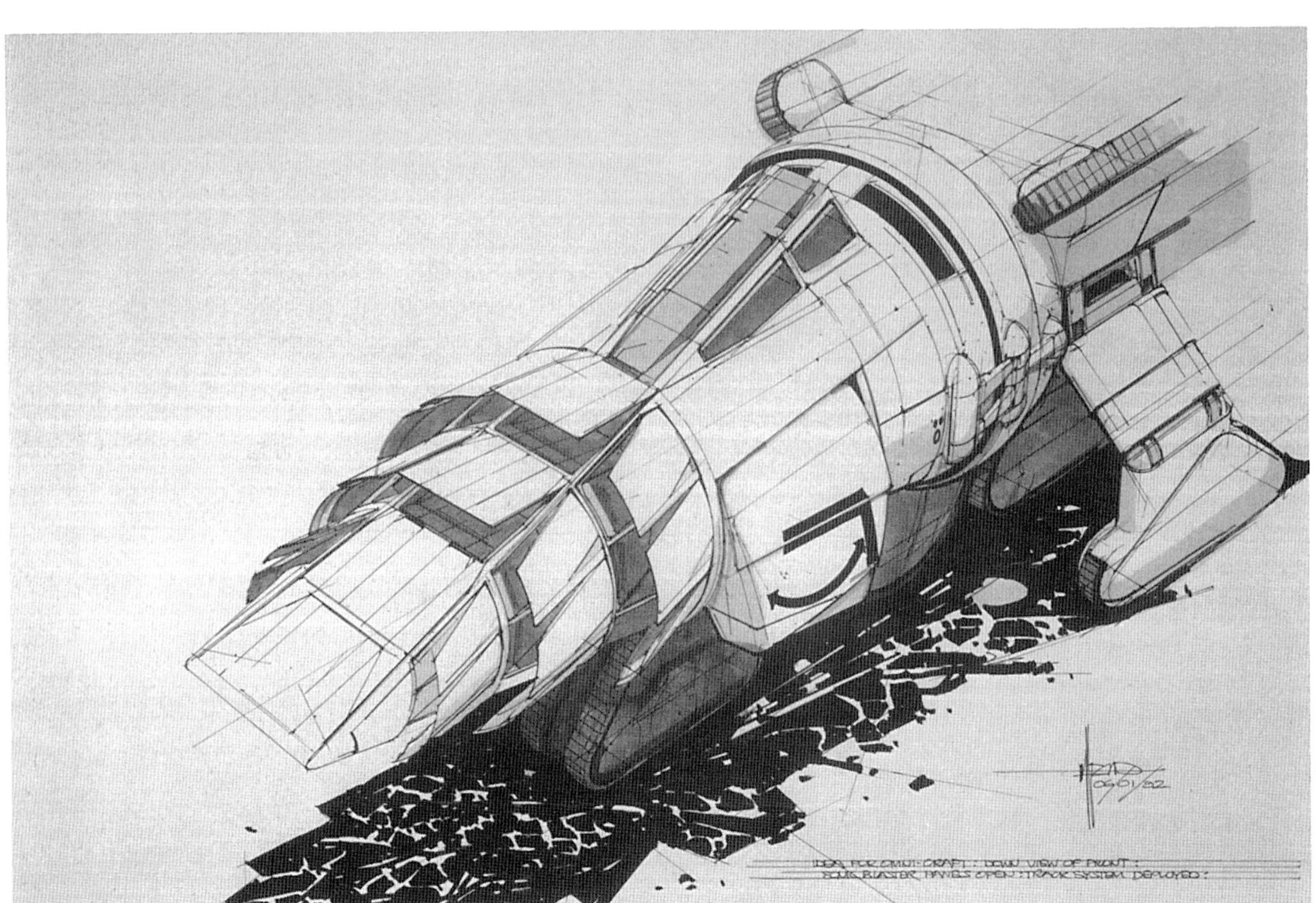
IDEA FOR SHUTTLE-CRAFT. DOWN VIEW OF FRONT.
SOLID BLASTER PANELS OPEN. TRACK SYSTEM DEPLOYED.

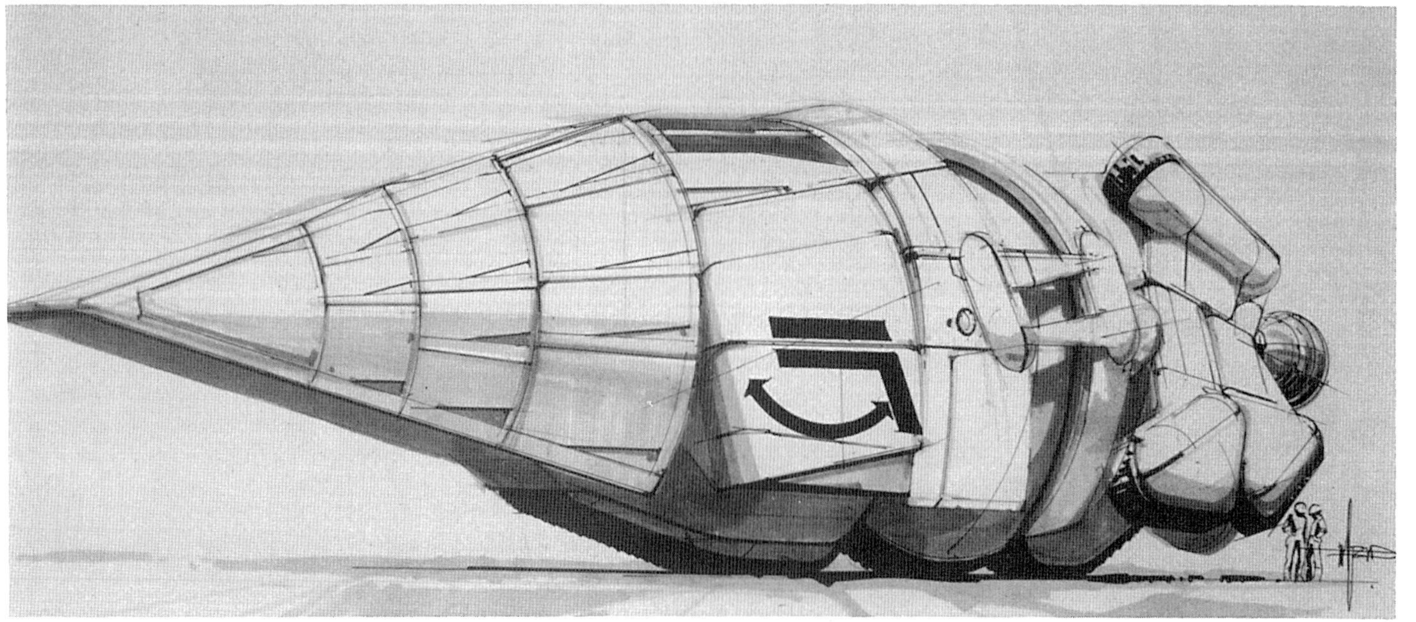

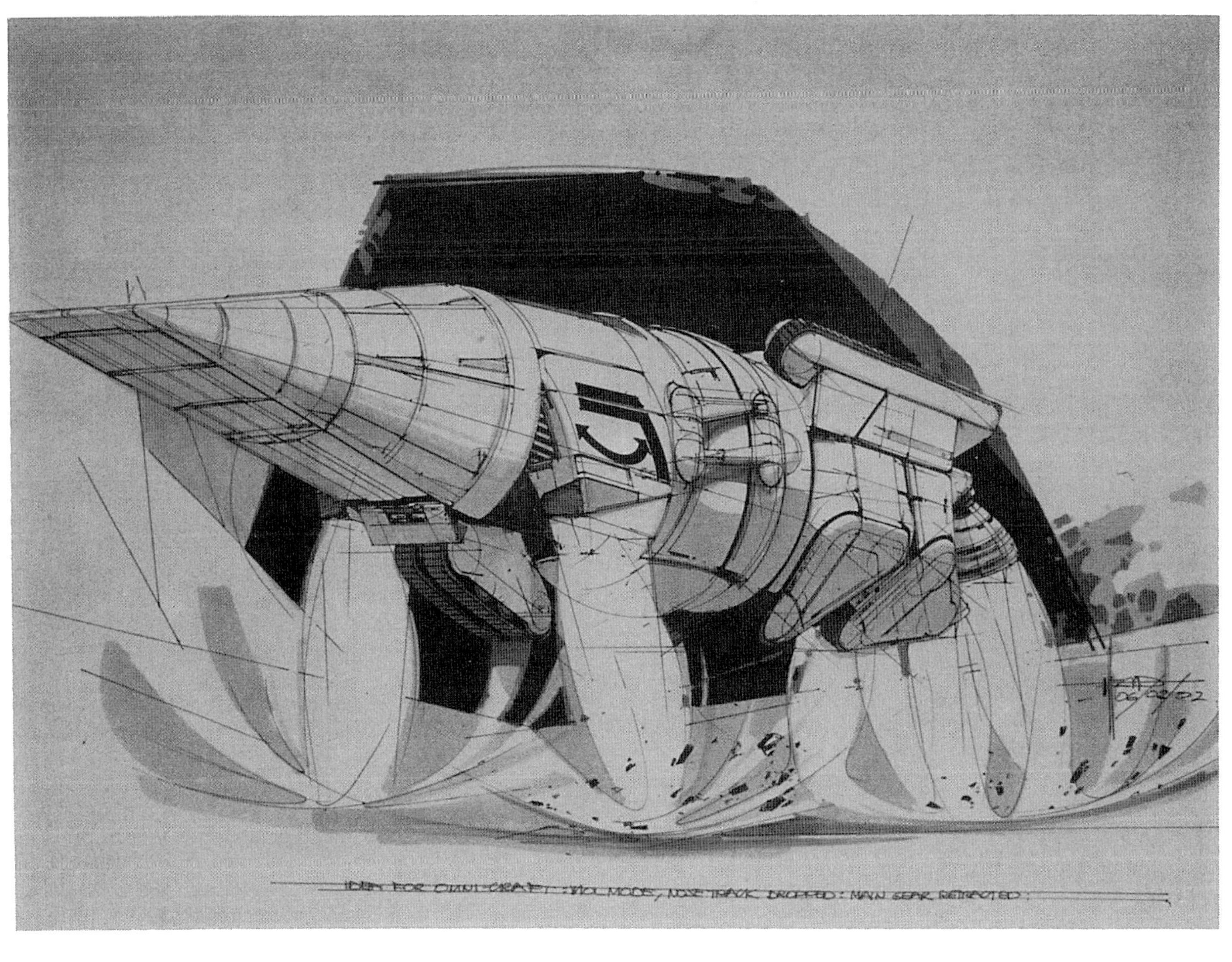

IDEA FOR OMNI-CRAFT : MOD MODE, NOSE TRACK DROPPED : MAIN GEAR RETRACTED


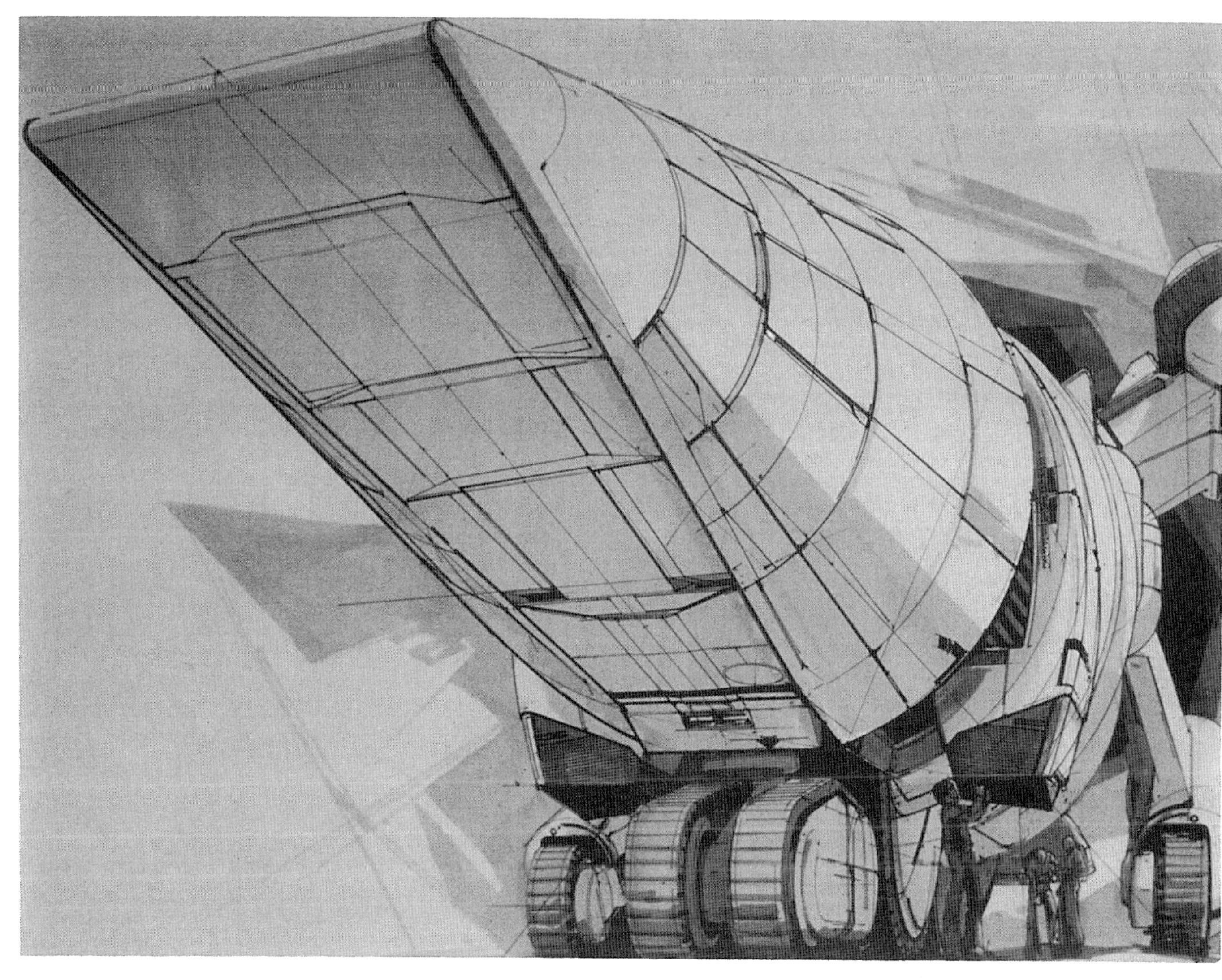

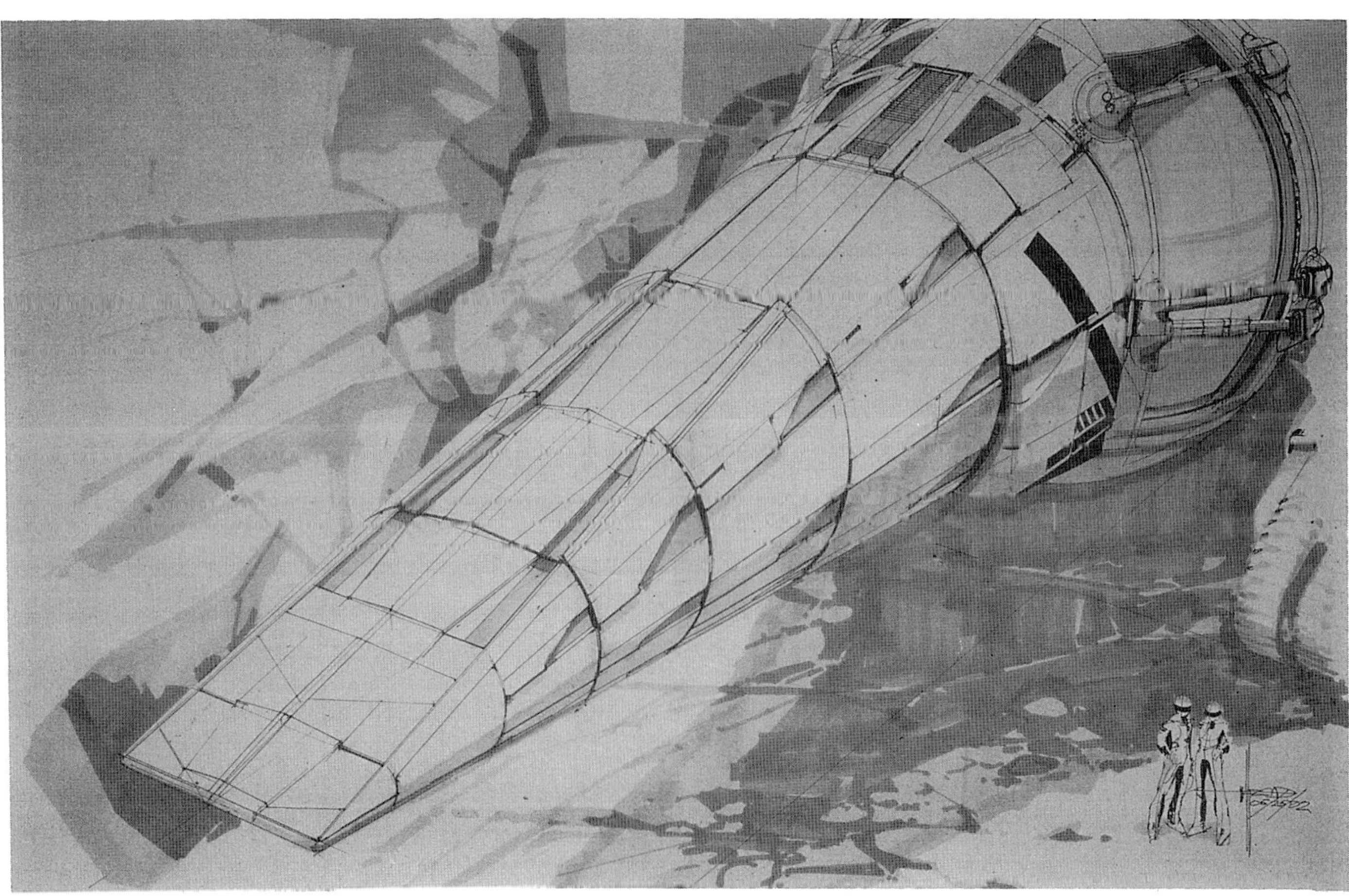

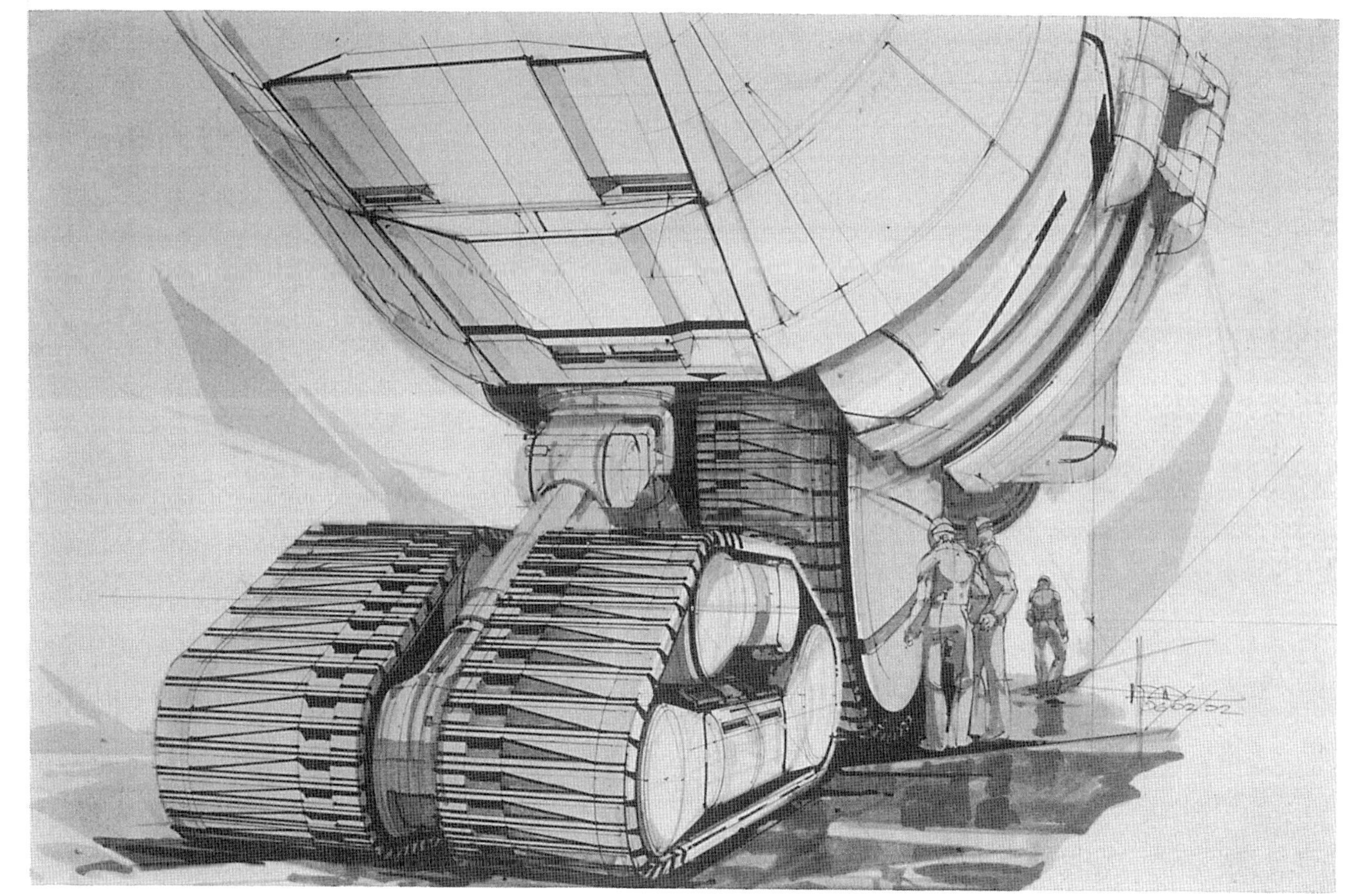

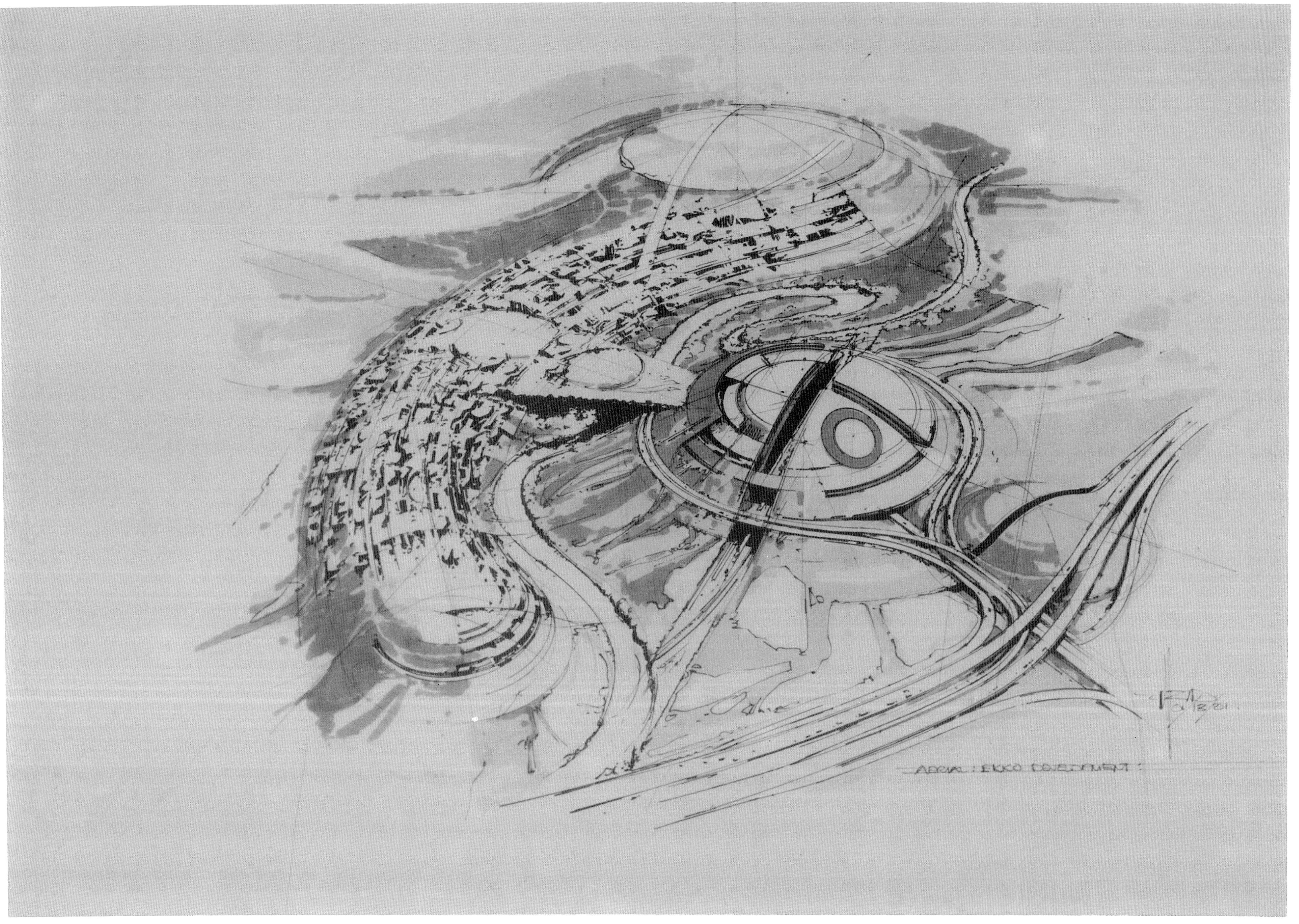
AERIAL : EKKO DEVELOPMENT

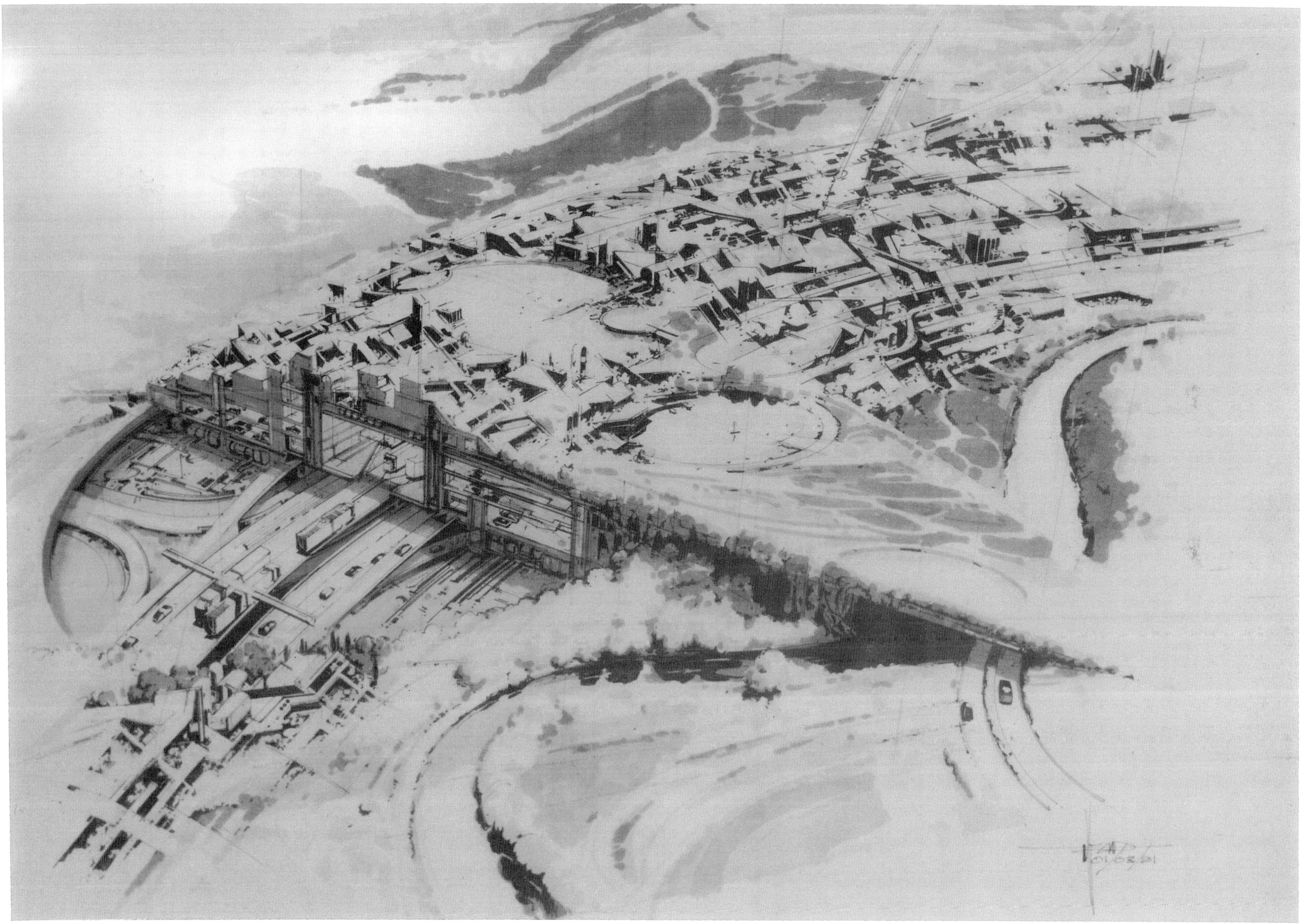

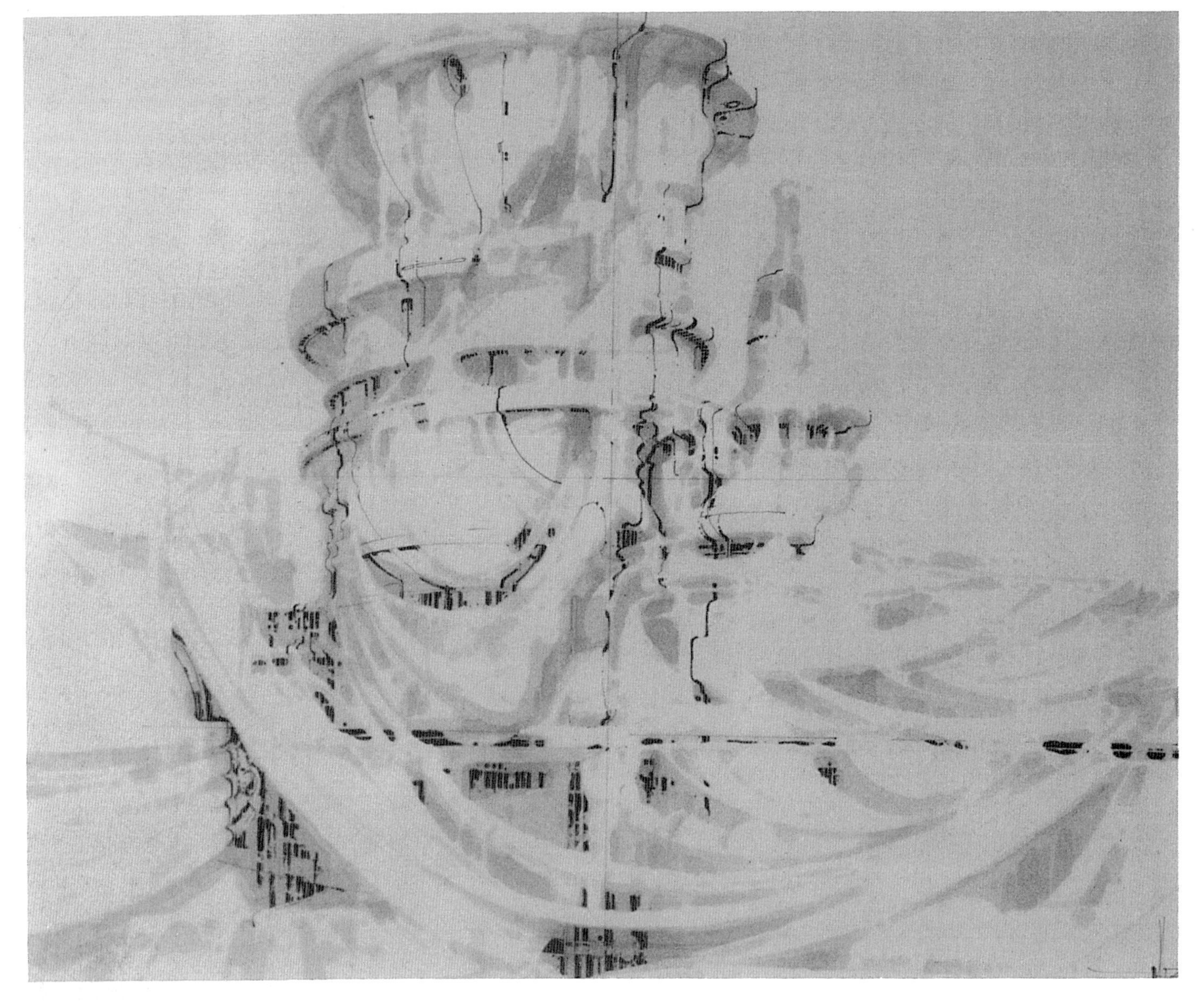

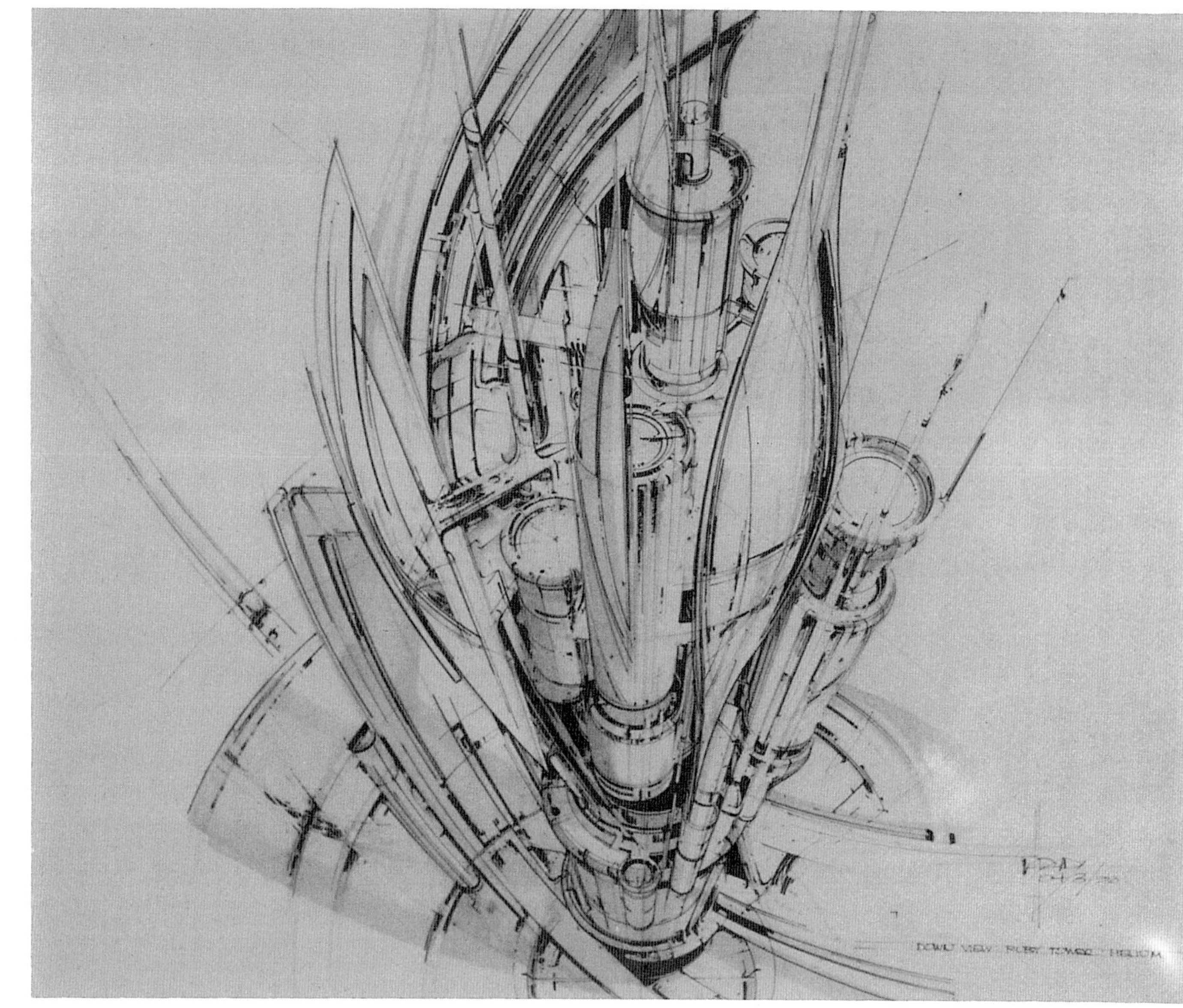

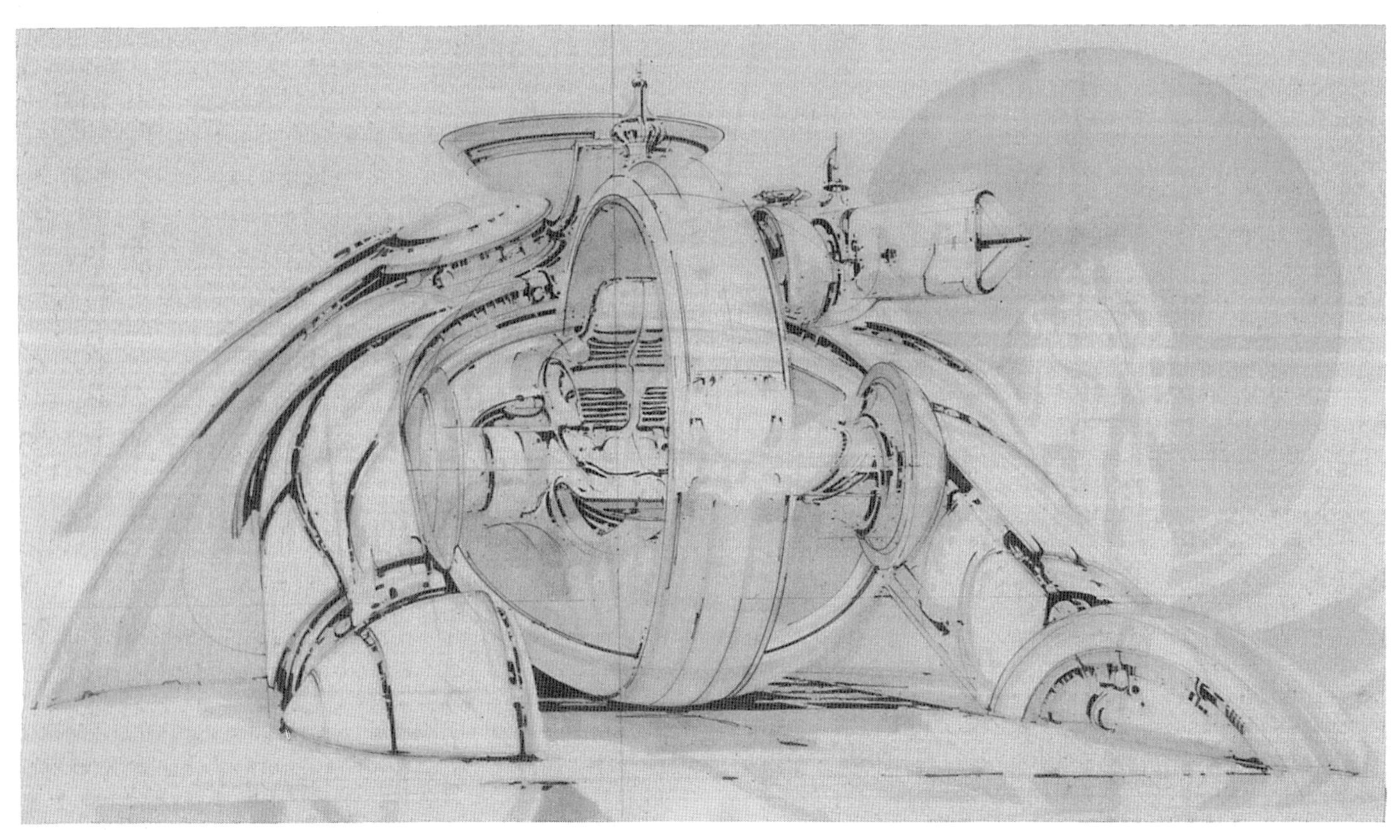

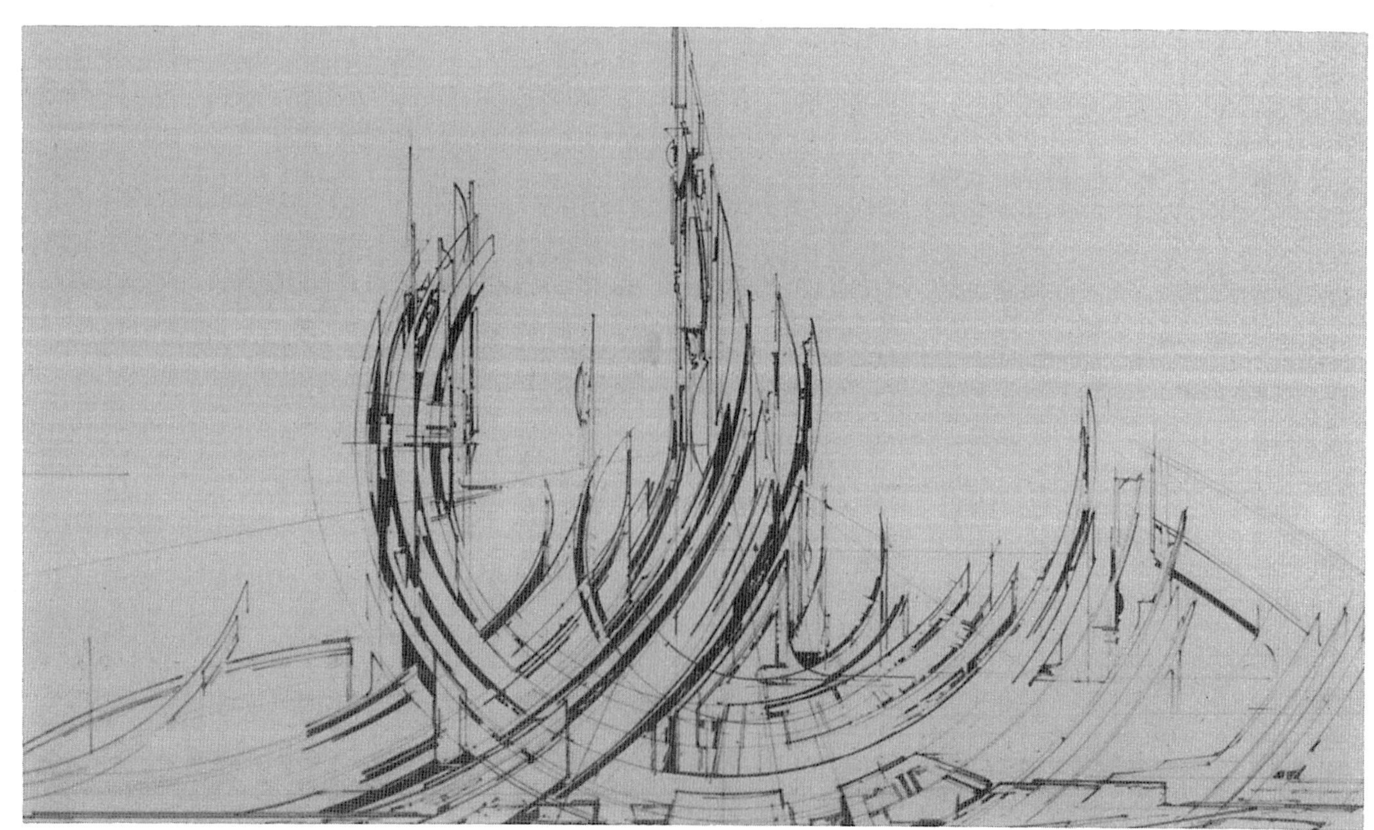

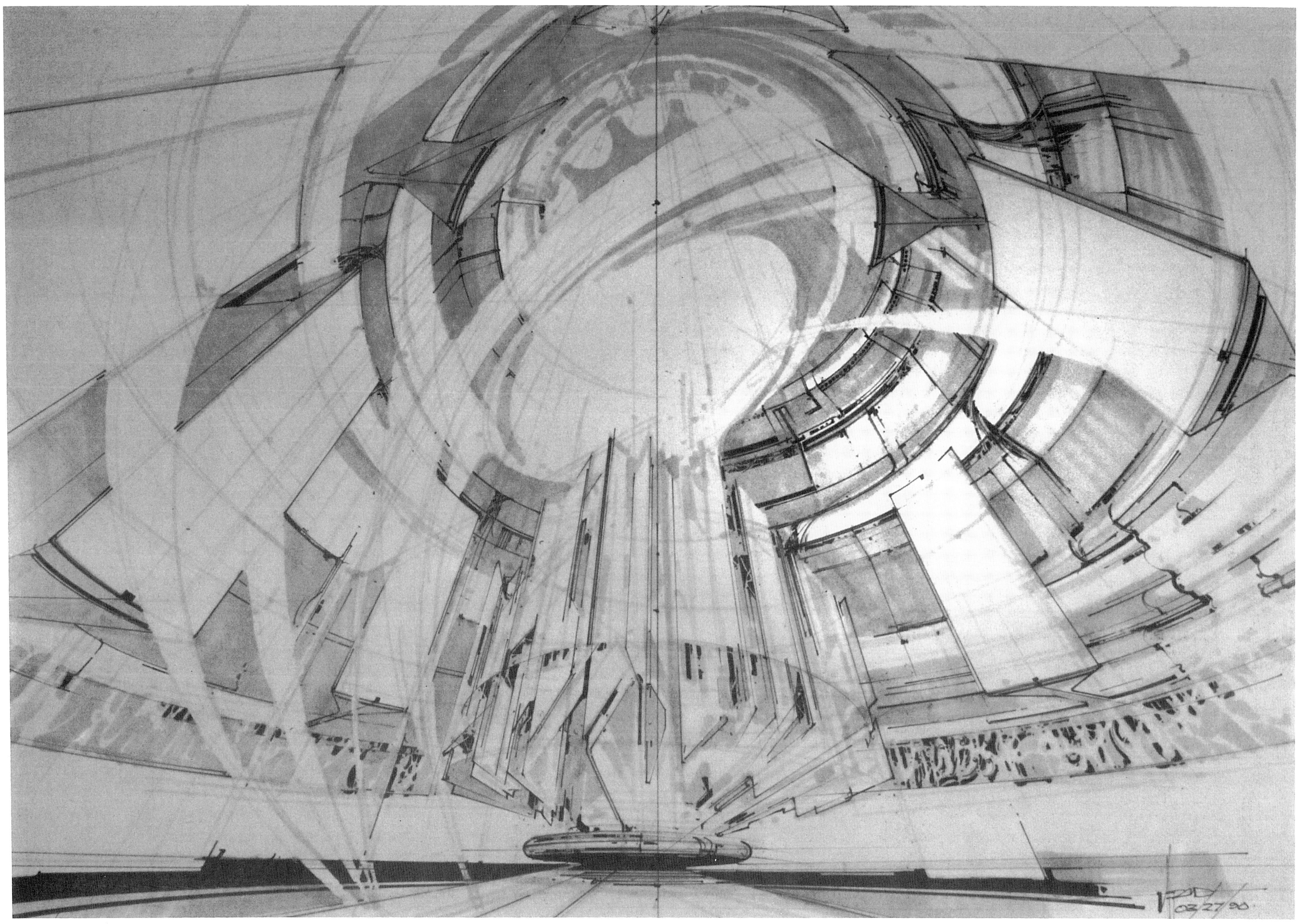

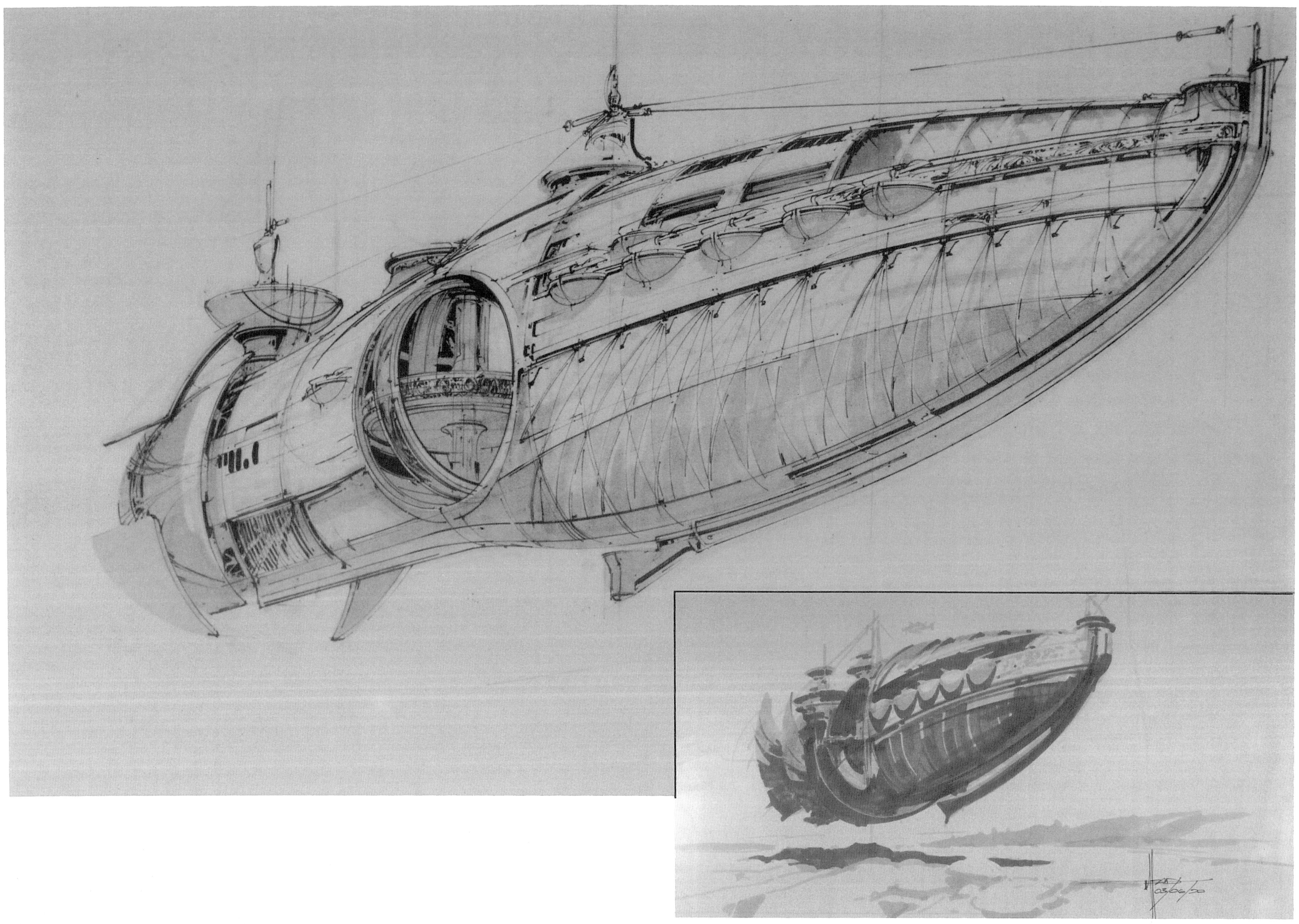

 ZADANGAN AIRSHIP PROPOSALS, "PRINCESS OF MARS"

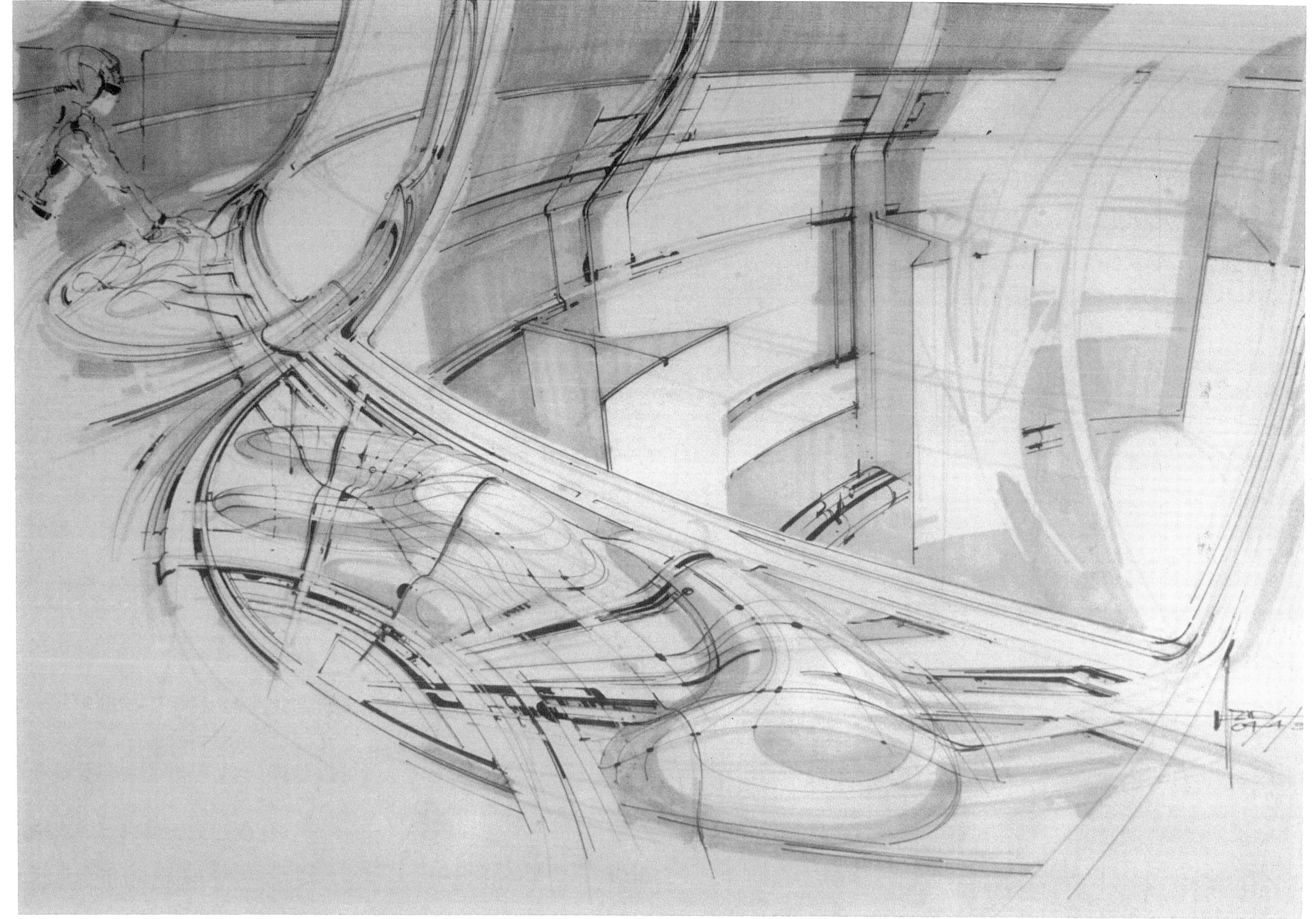

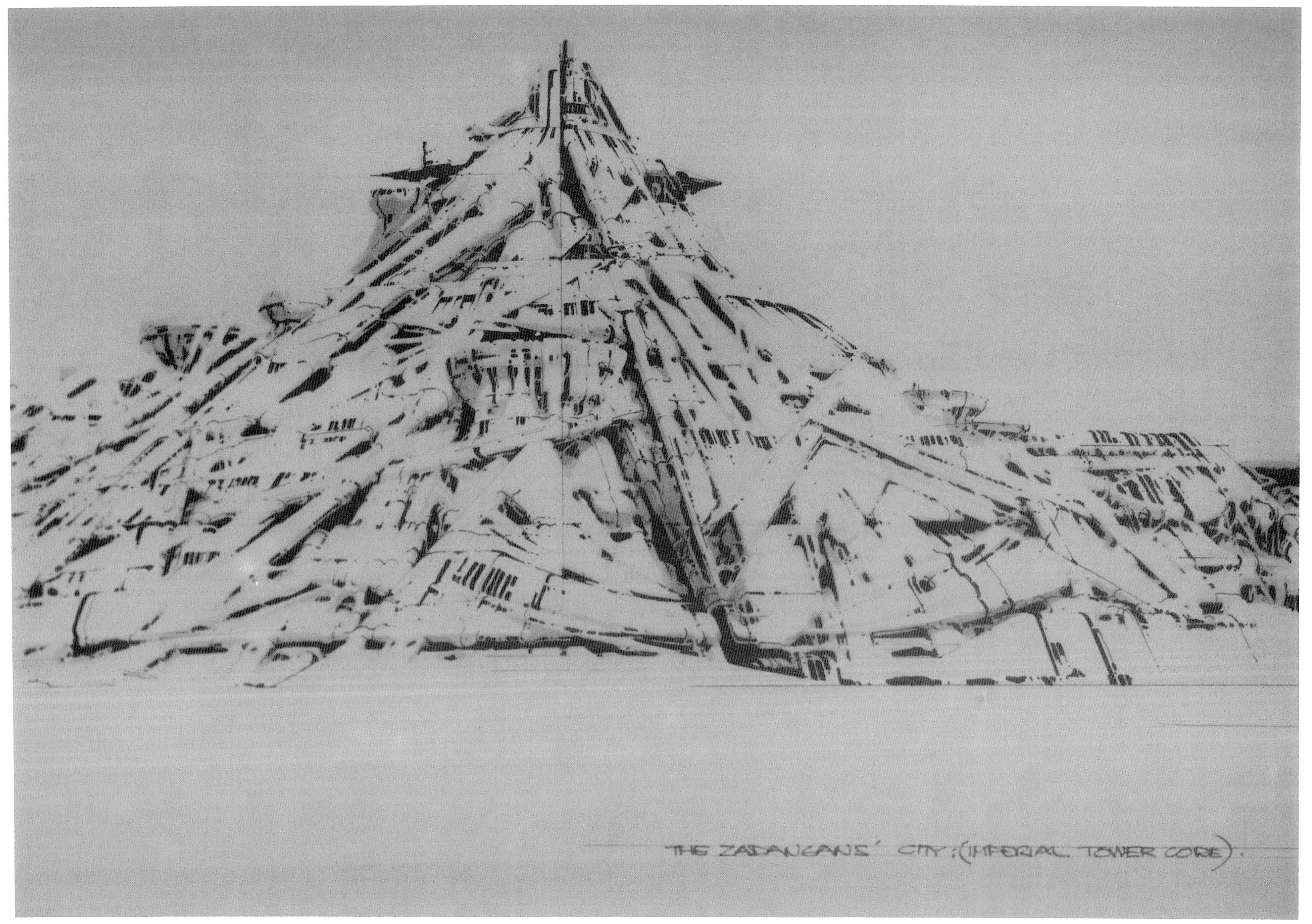
THE ZADANGANS' CITY : (IMPERIAL TOWER CORE).

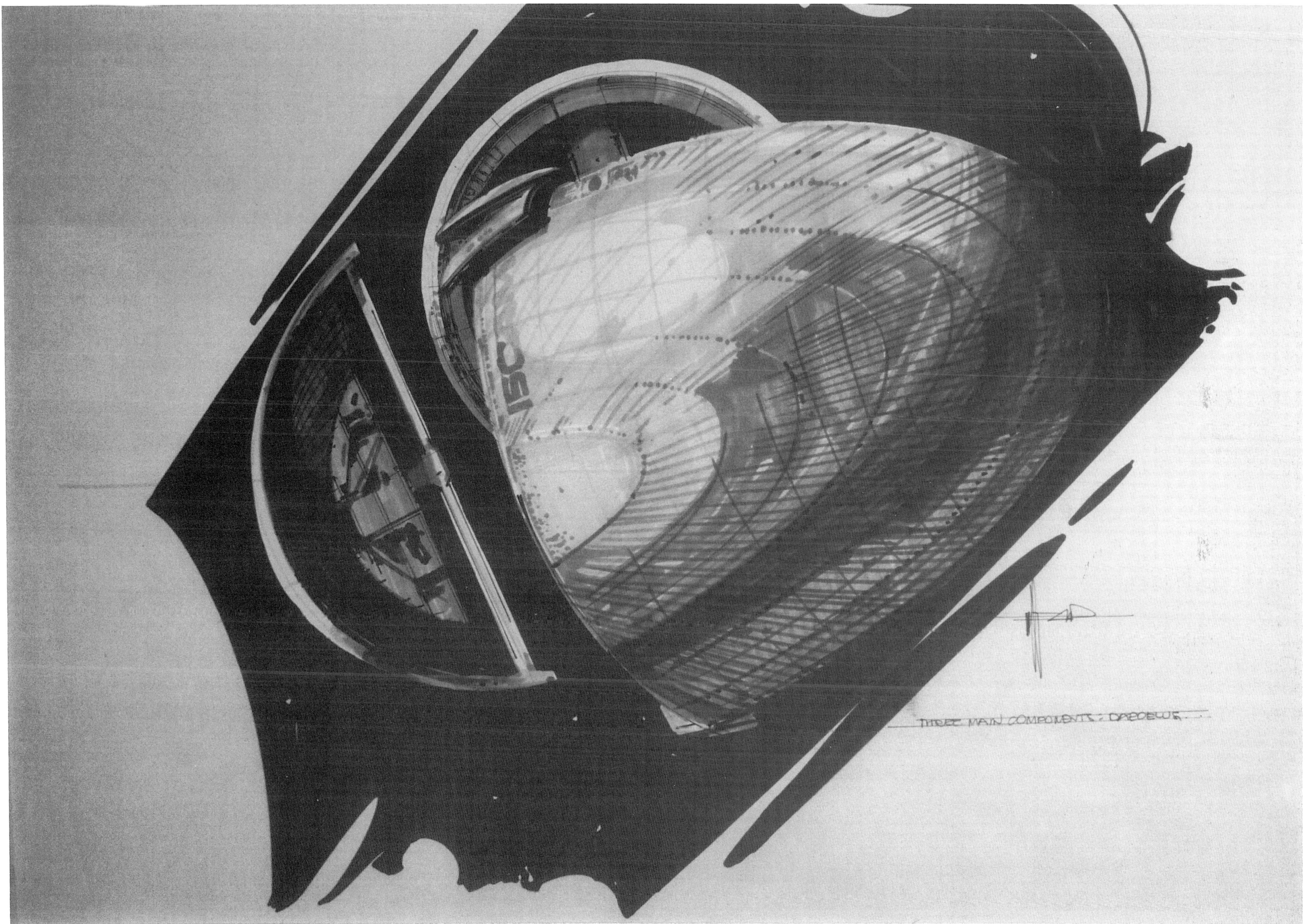

ISC
THREE MAIN COMPONENTS: DAEDELUS

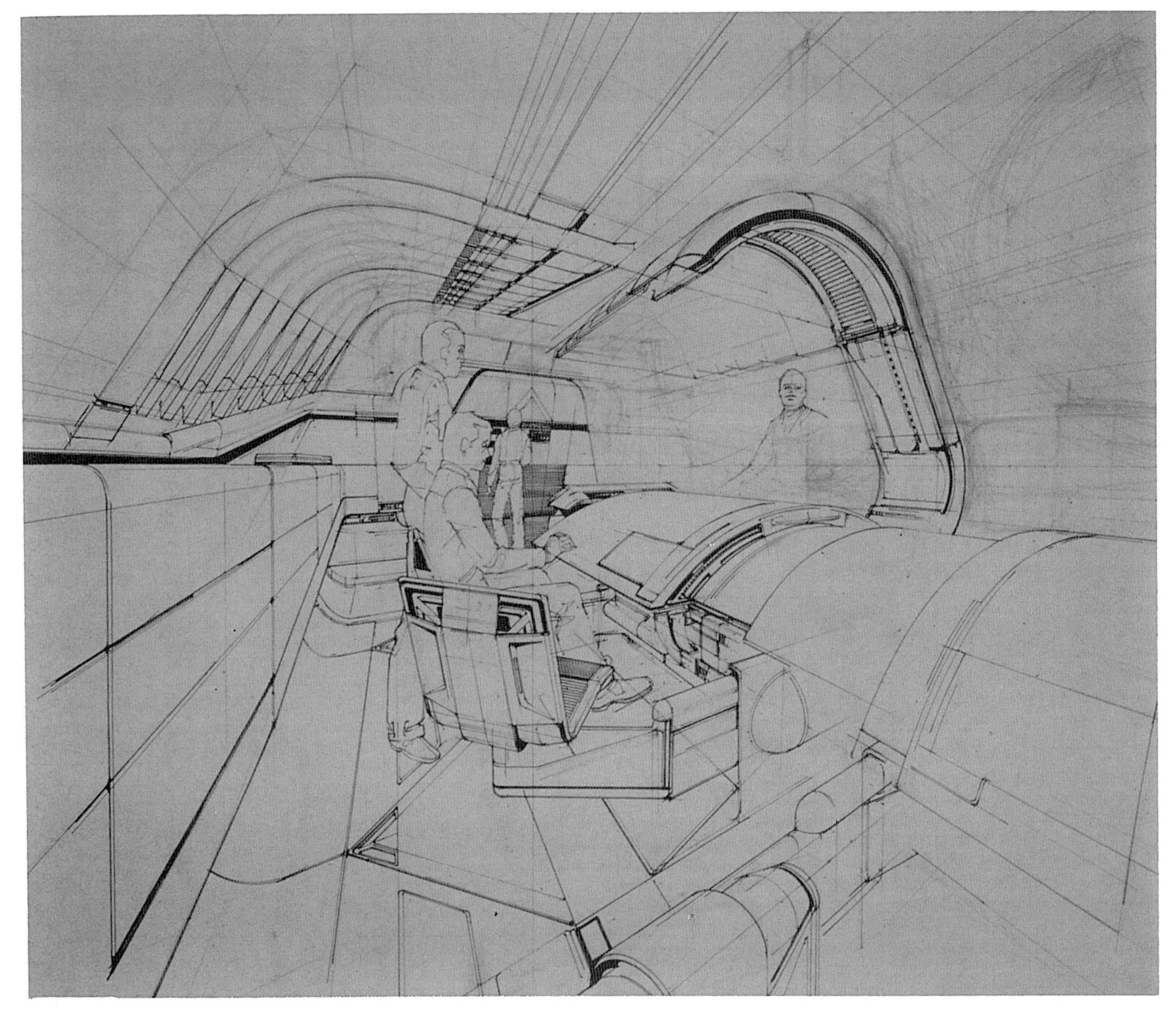

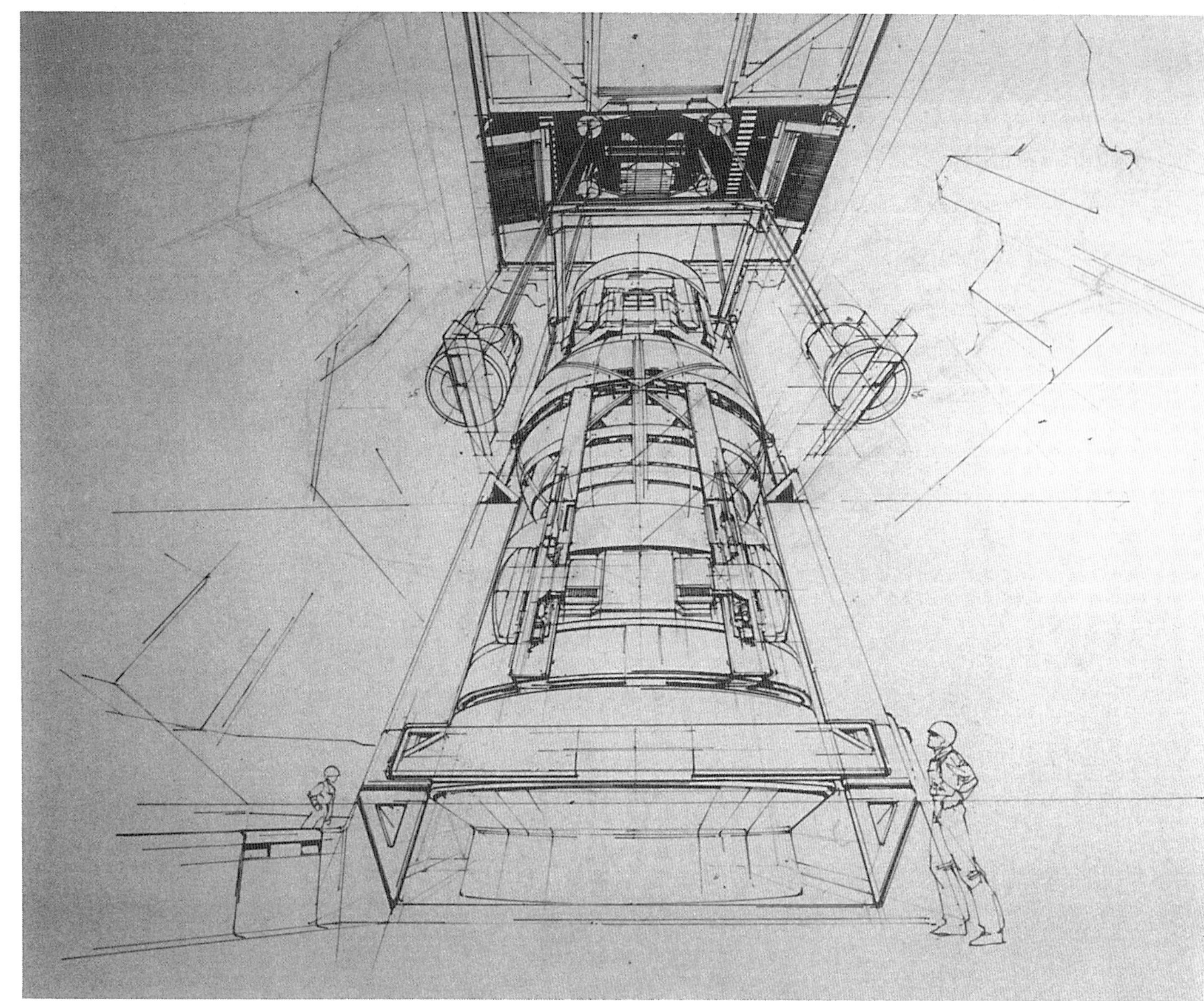

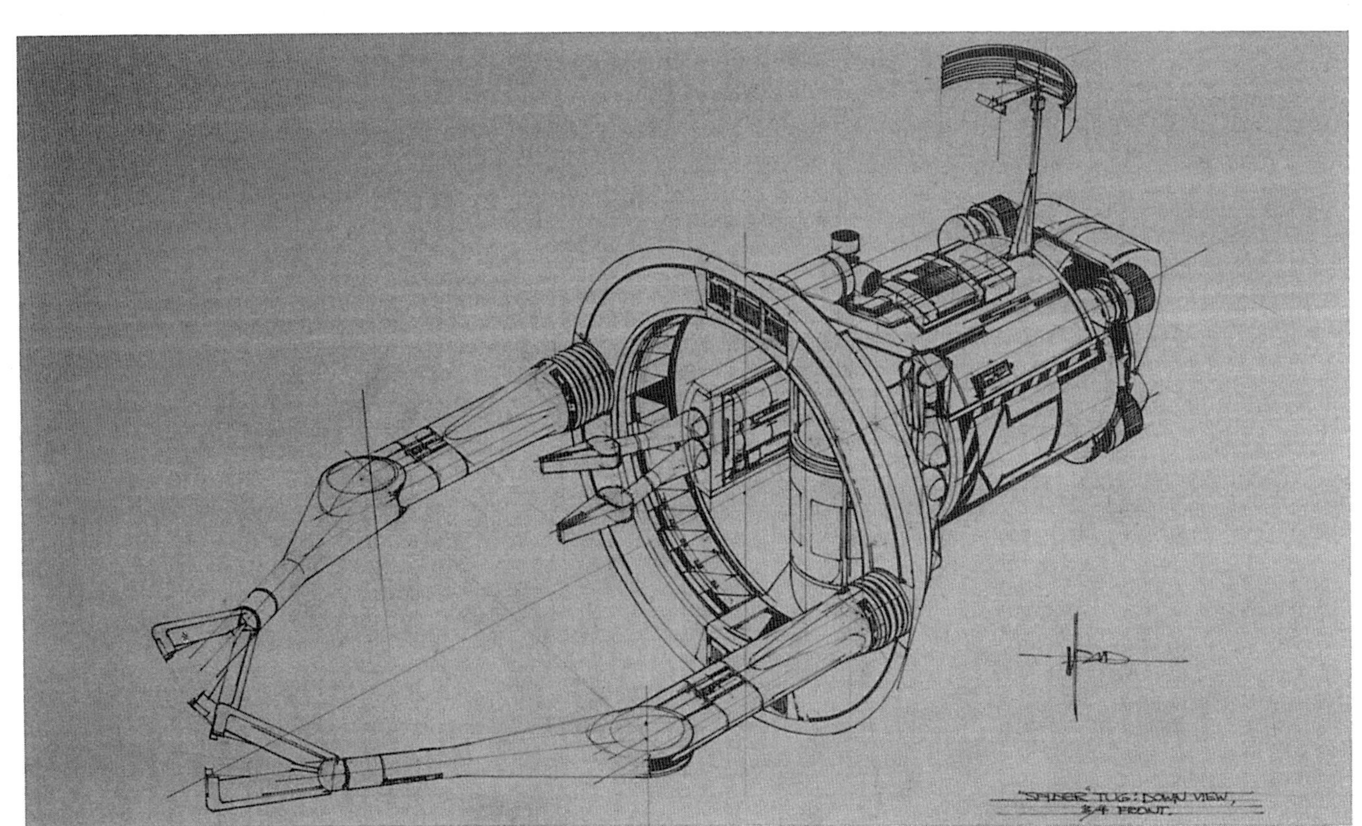

"SPIDER TUG : DOWN VIEW,
3/4 FRONT.


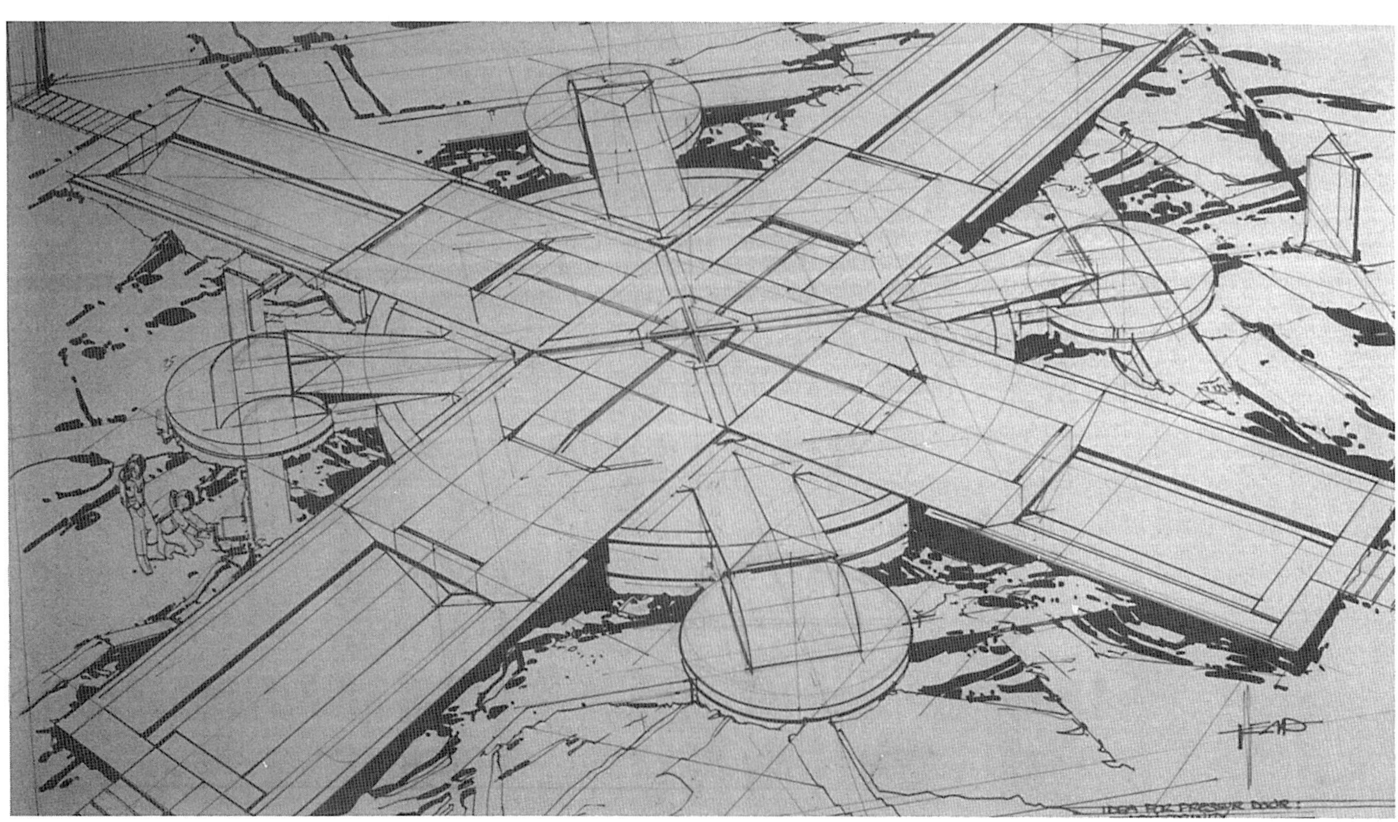

IDEA FOR PRESSURE DOOR:

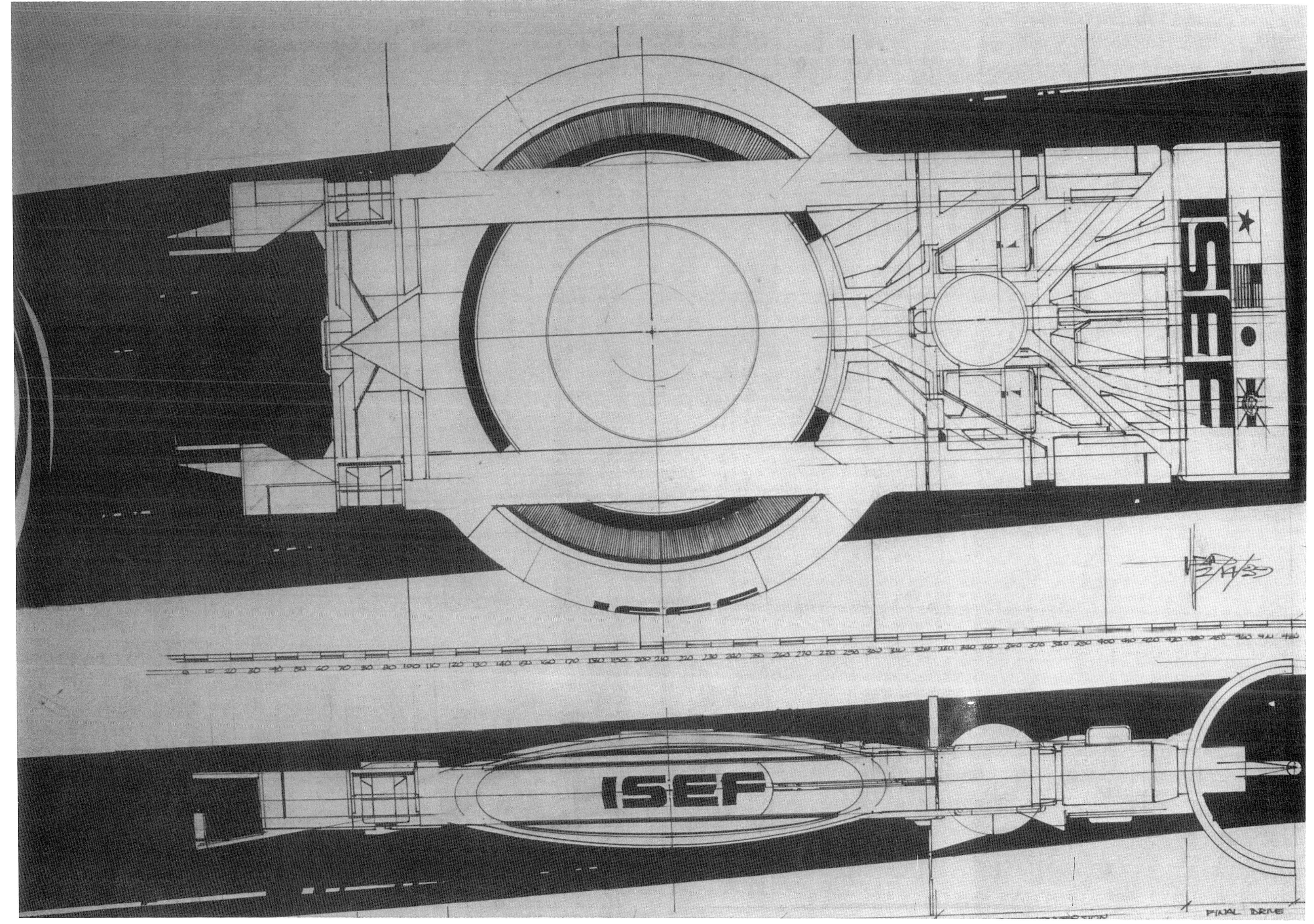

ISEF
ISEF
FINAL DRIVE

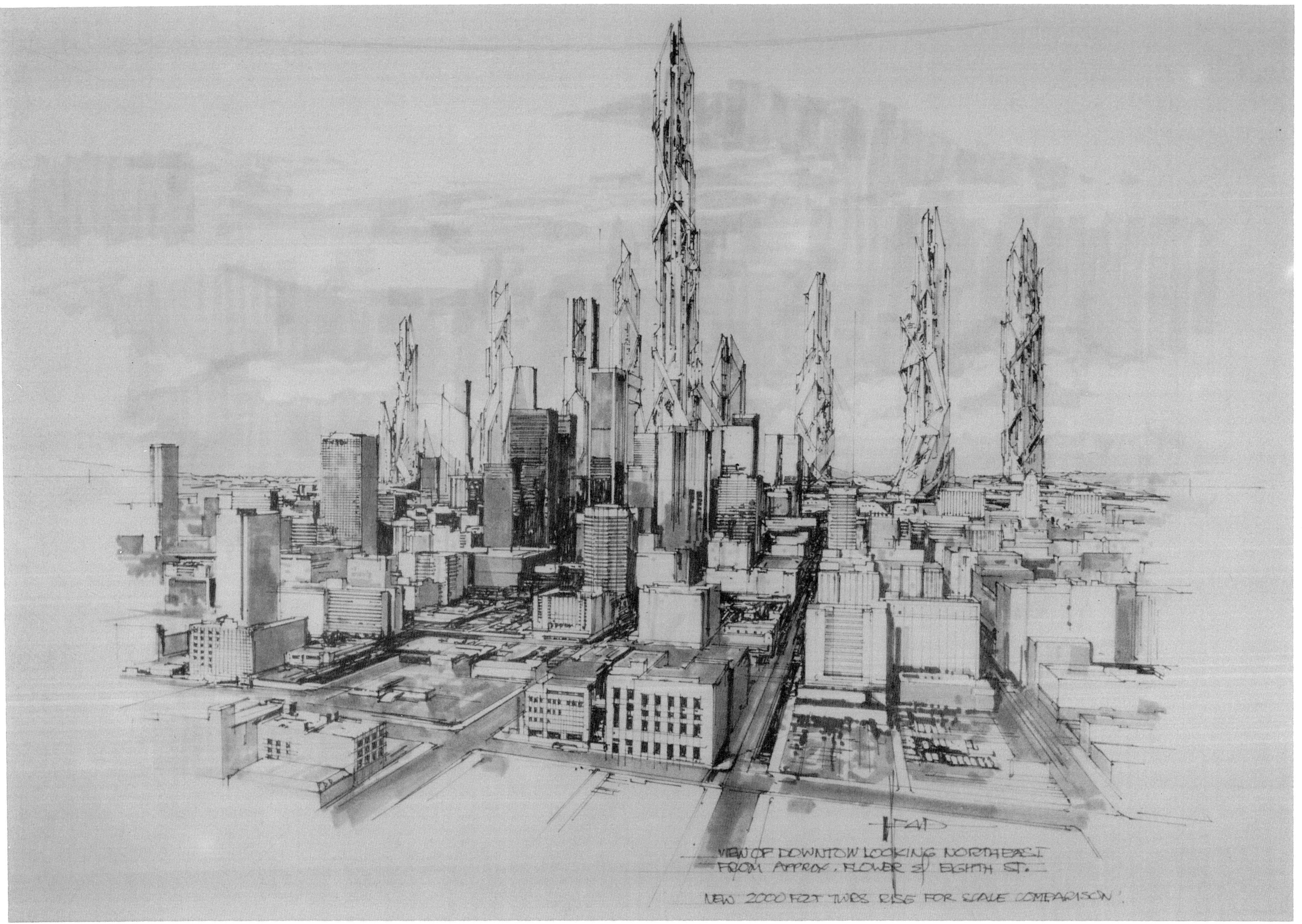

VIEW OF DOWNTOW LOOKING NORTHEAST
FROM APPROX. FLOWER & EIGHTH ST.
NEW 2000 FOOT TWRS RISE FOR SCALE COMPARISON

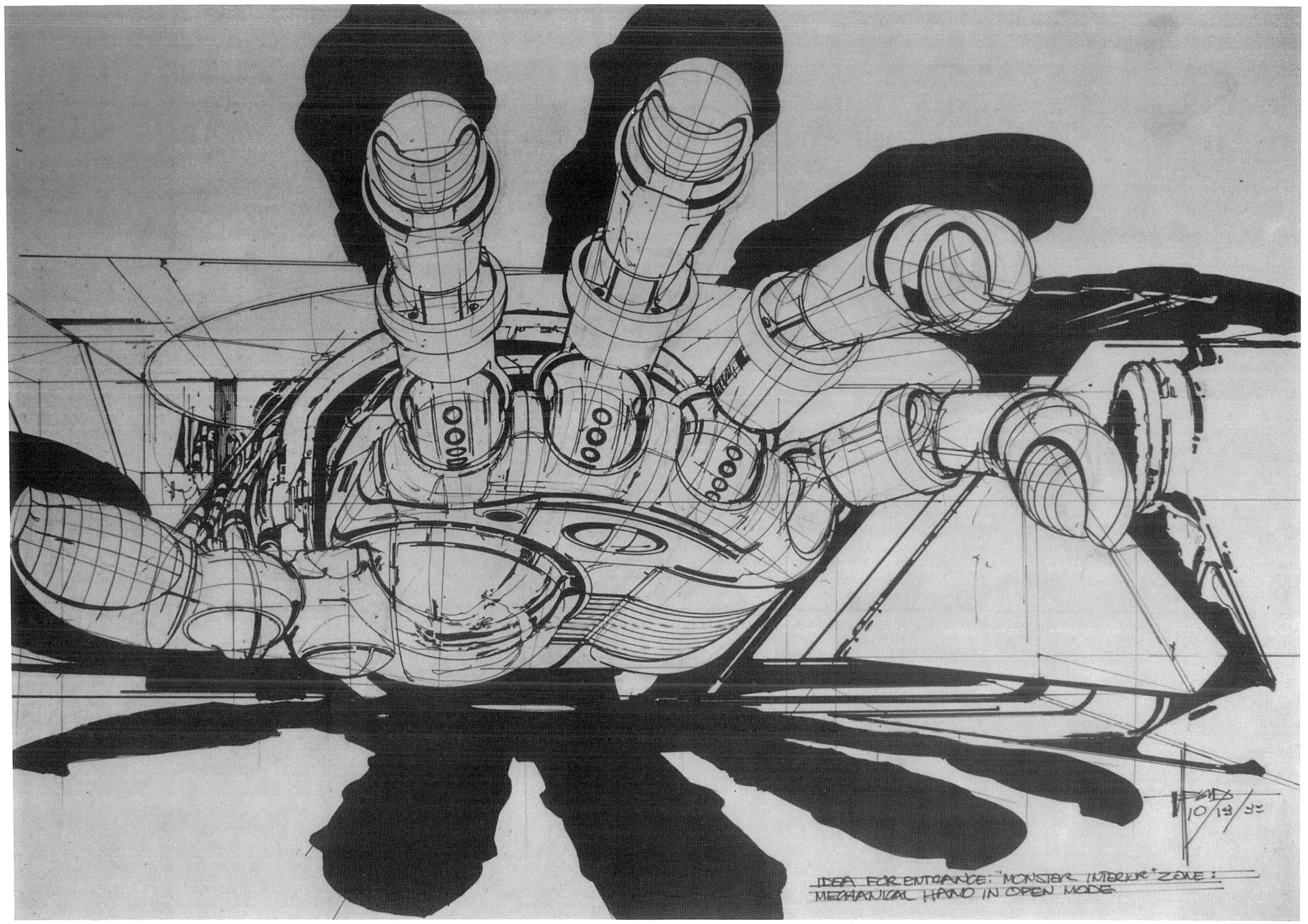

IDEA FOR ENTRANCE: "MONSTER INTERIOR" ZONE:
MECHANICAL HAND IN OPEN MODE
10/18/92

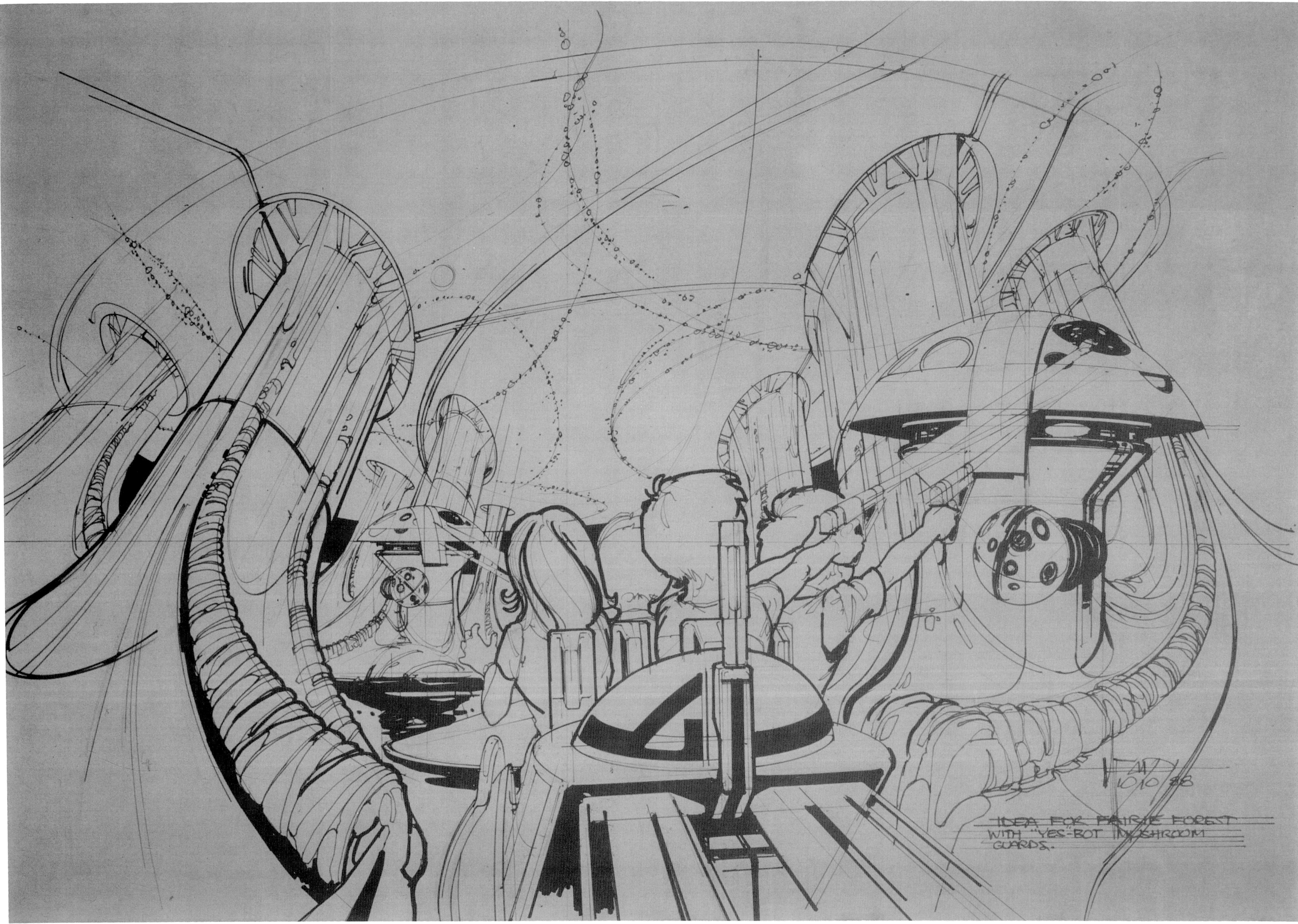

IDEA FOR FAERIE FOREST
WITH "YES-BOT" MUSHROOM
GUARDS.

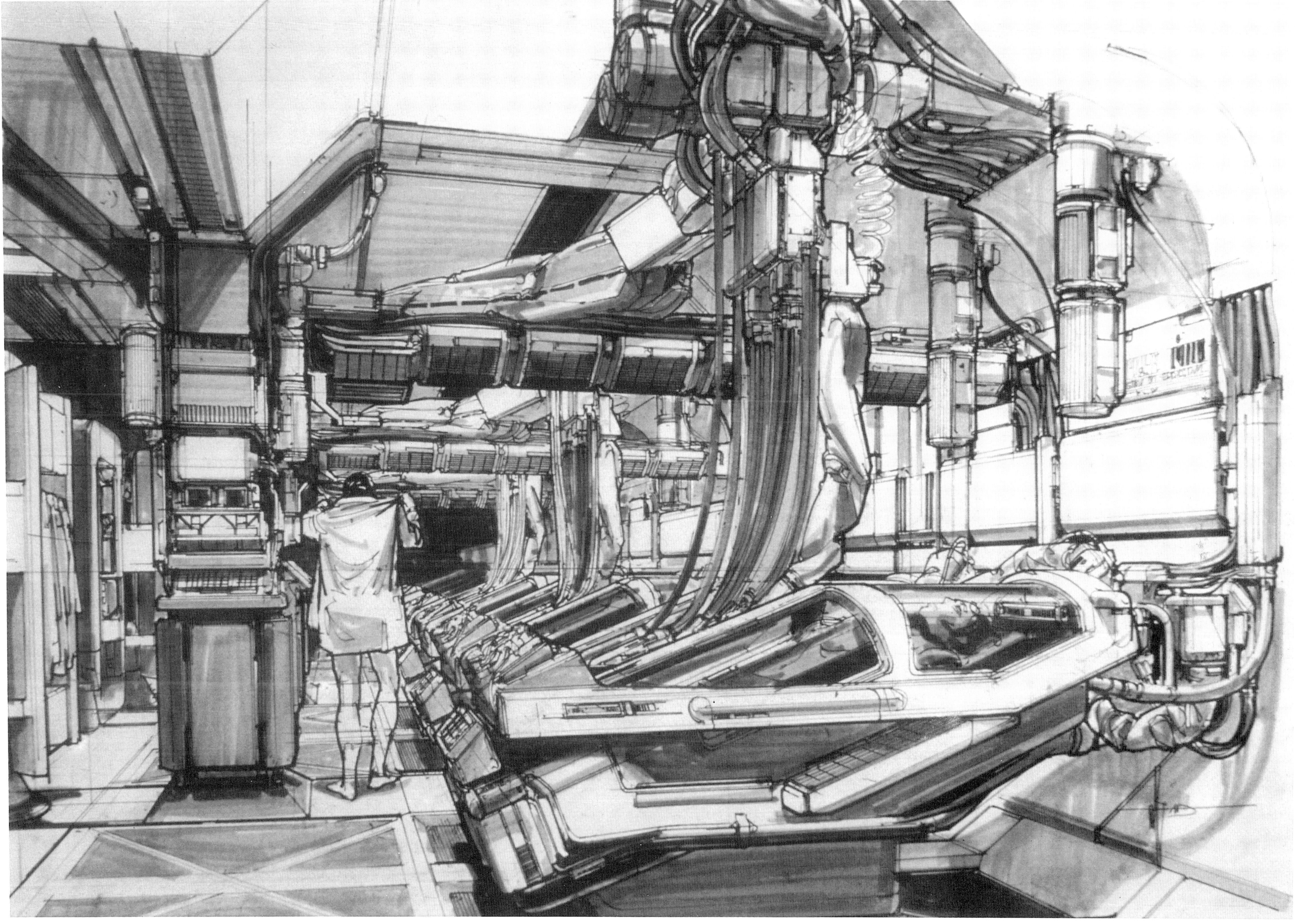

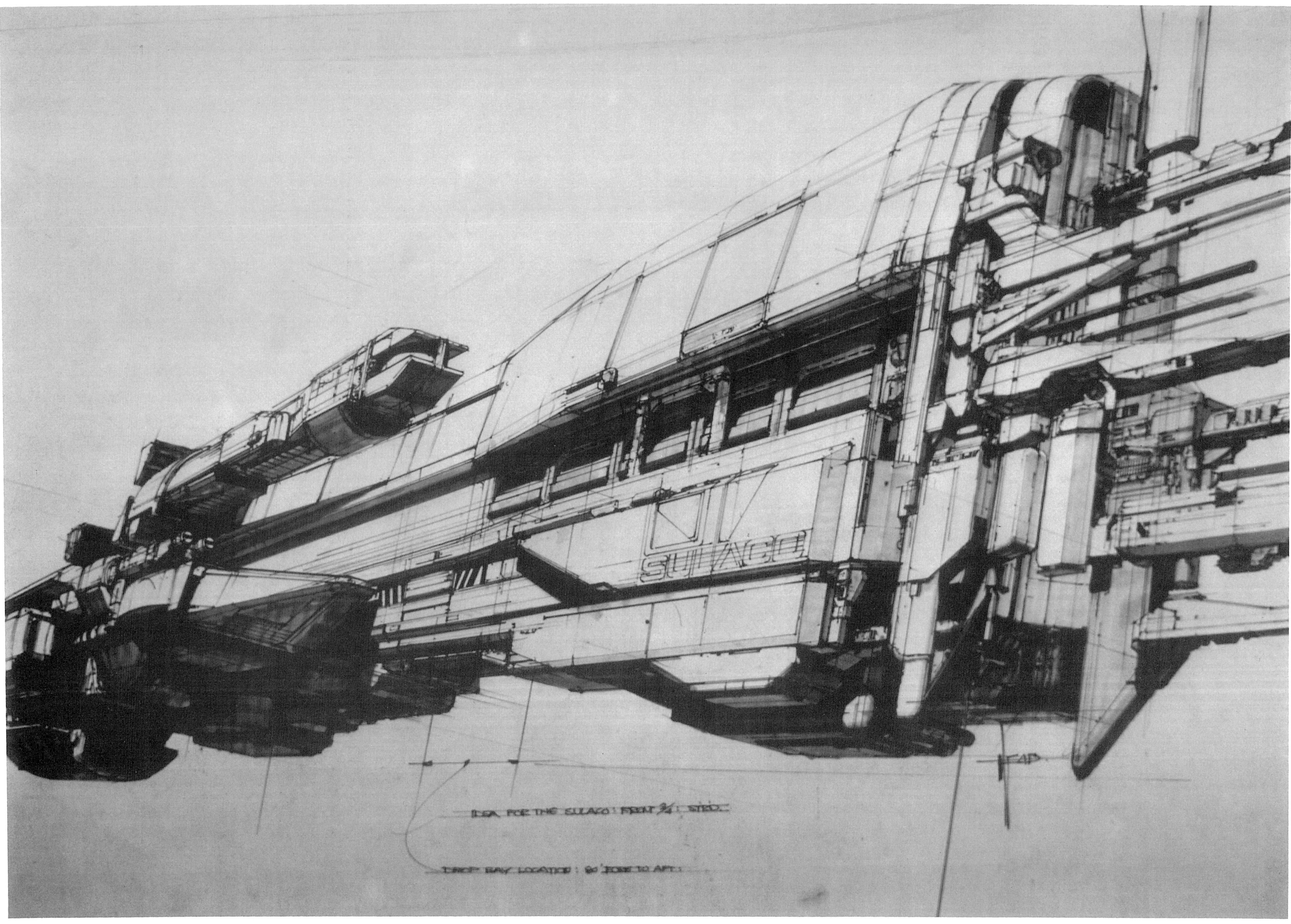

SULACO
IDEA FOR THE SULACO: FRONT 3/4 STBD.
DROP BAY LOCATION: 80' FORE TO AFT.

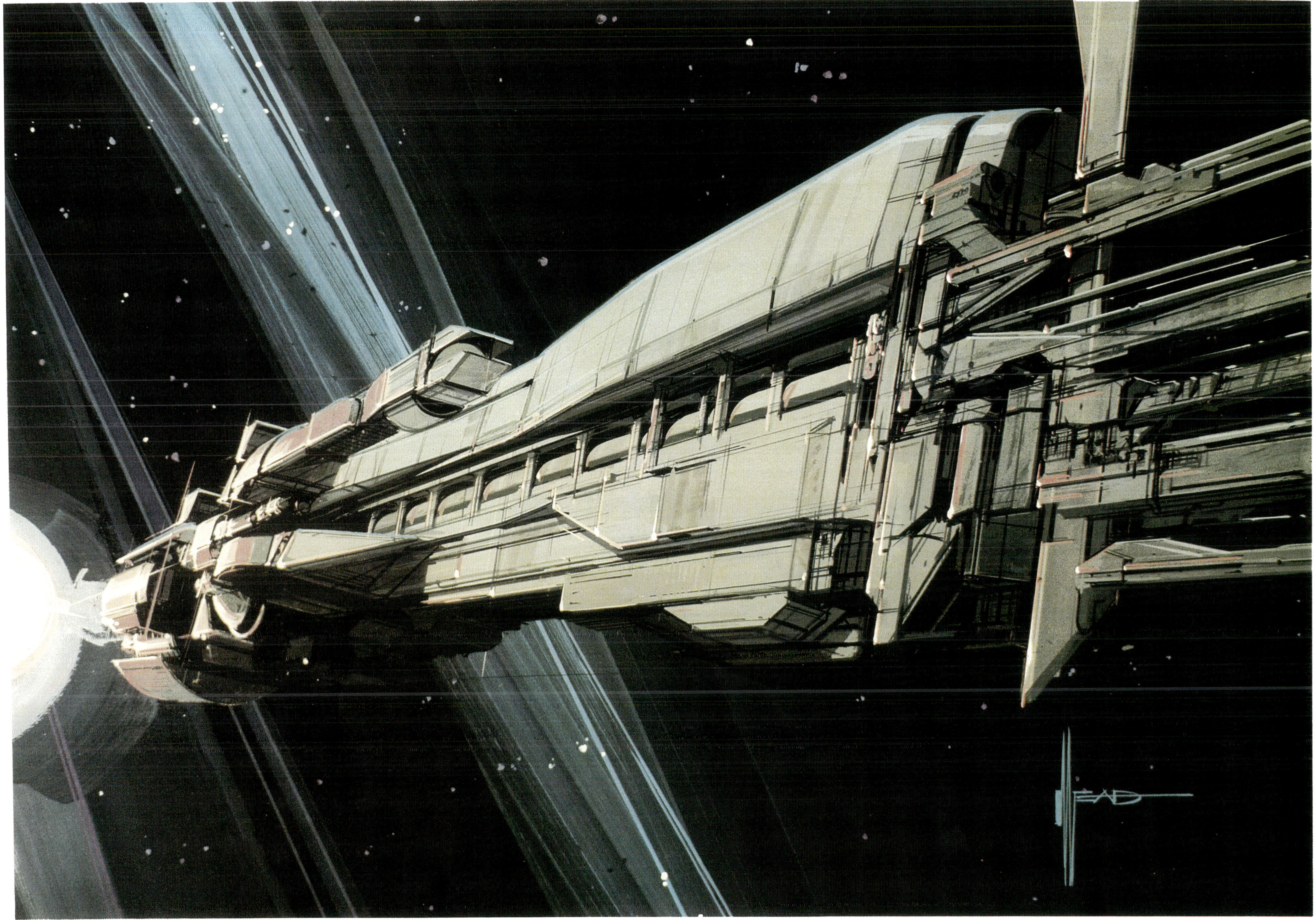

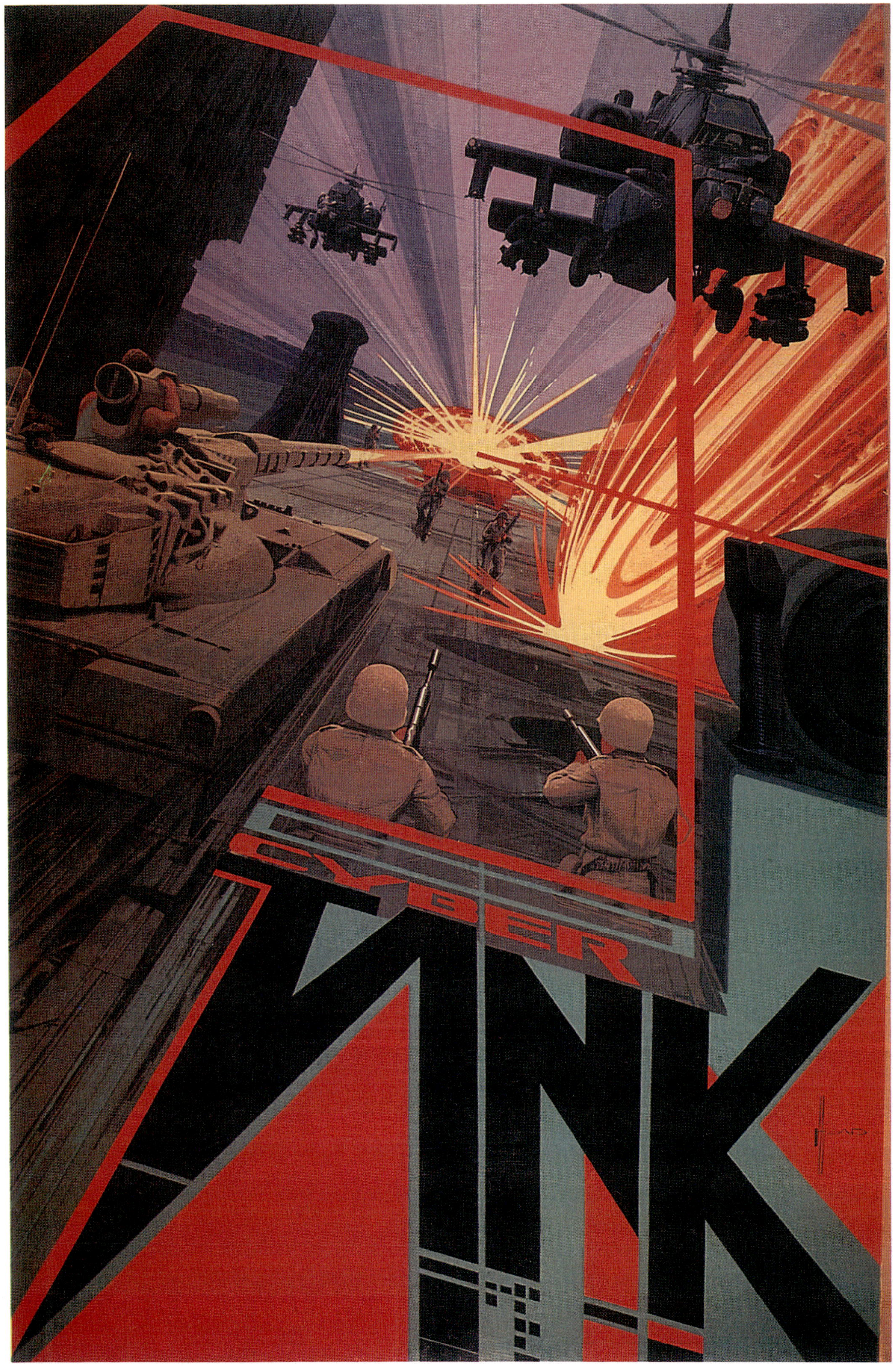

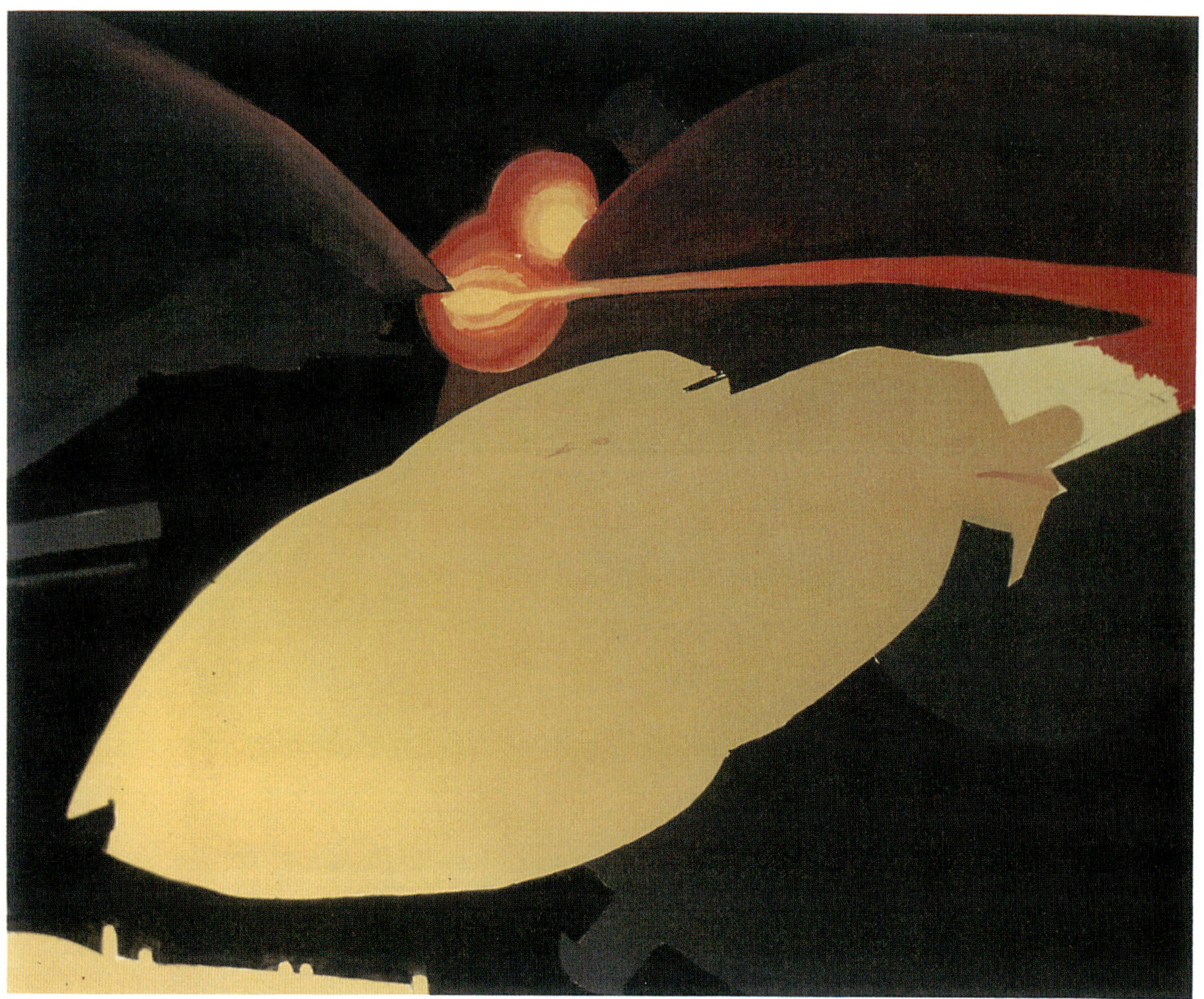

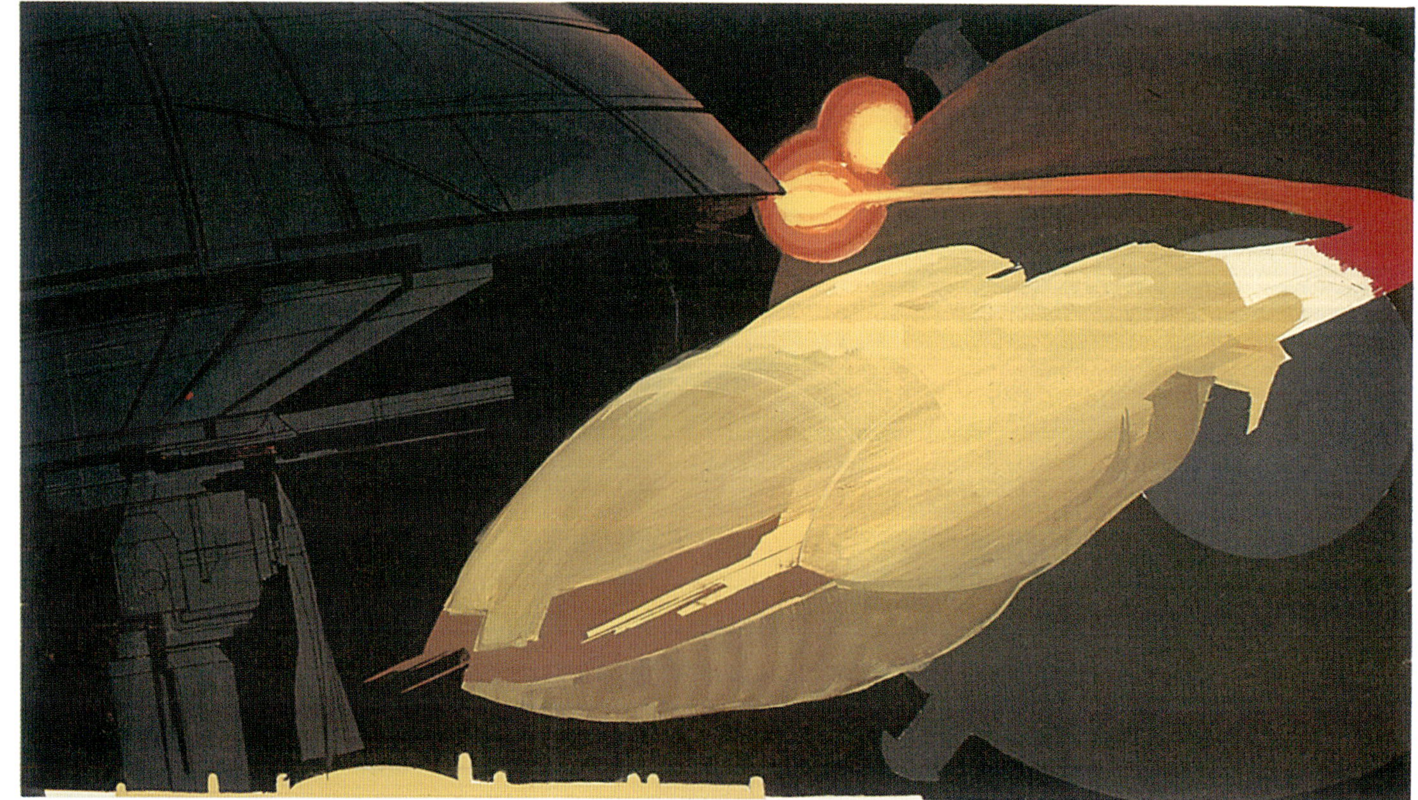

SPACESHIP 2056 PRELIMINARIES

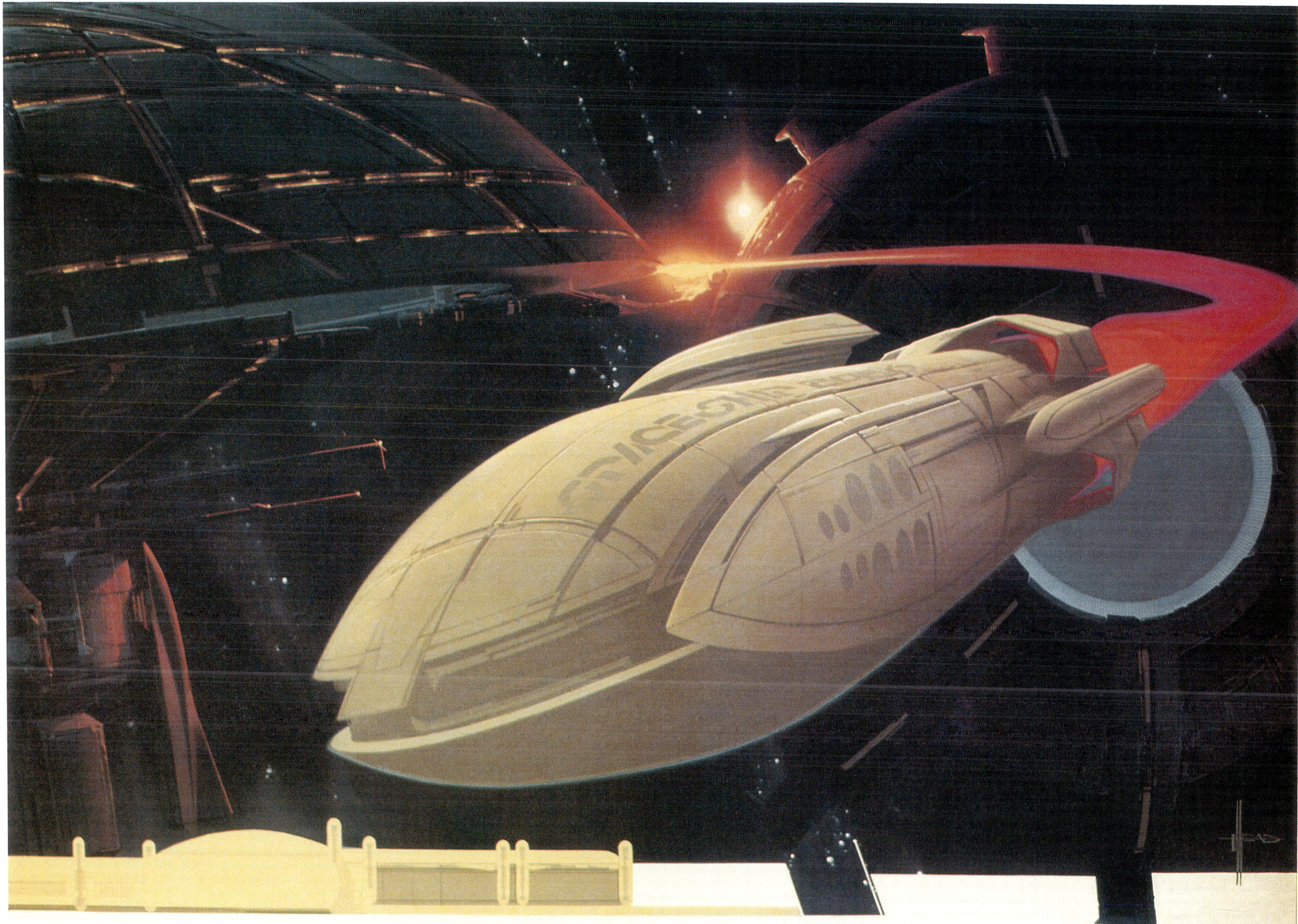
SPACESHIP

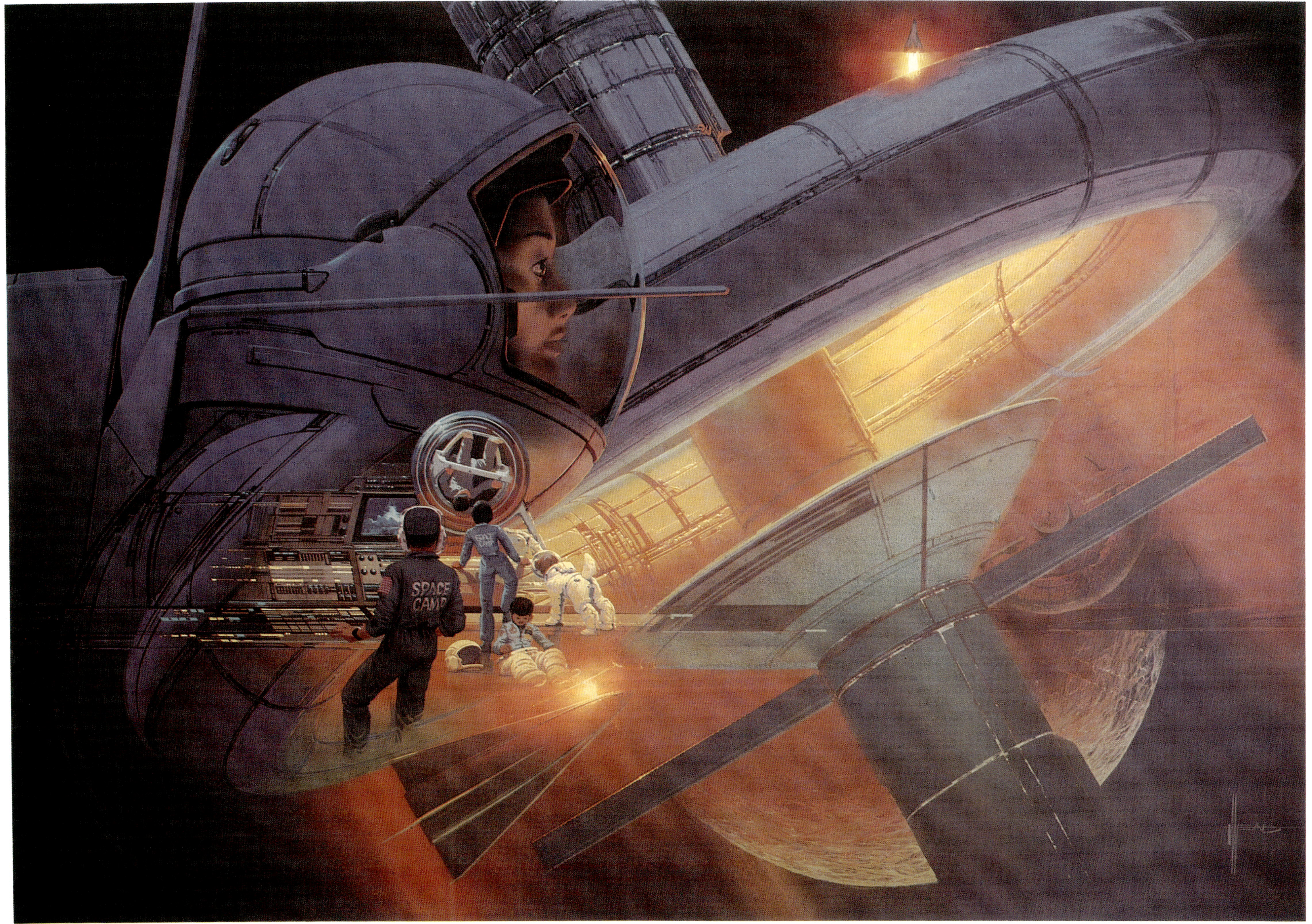

SPACE
CAMP

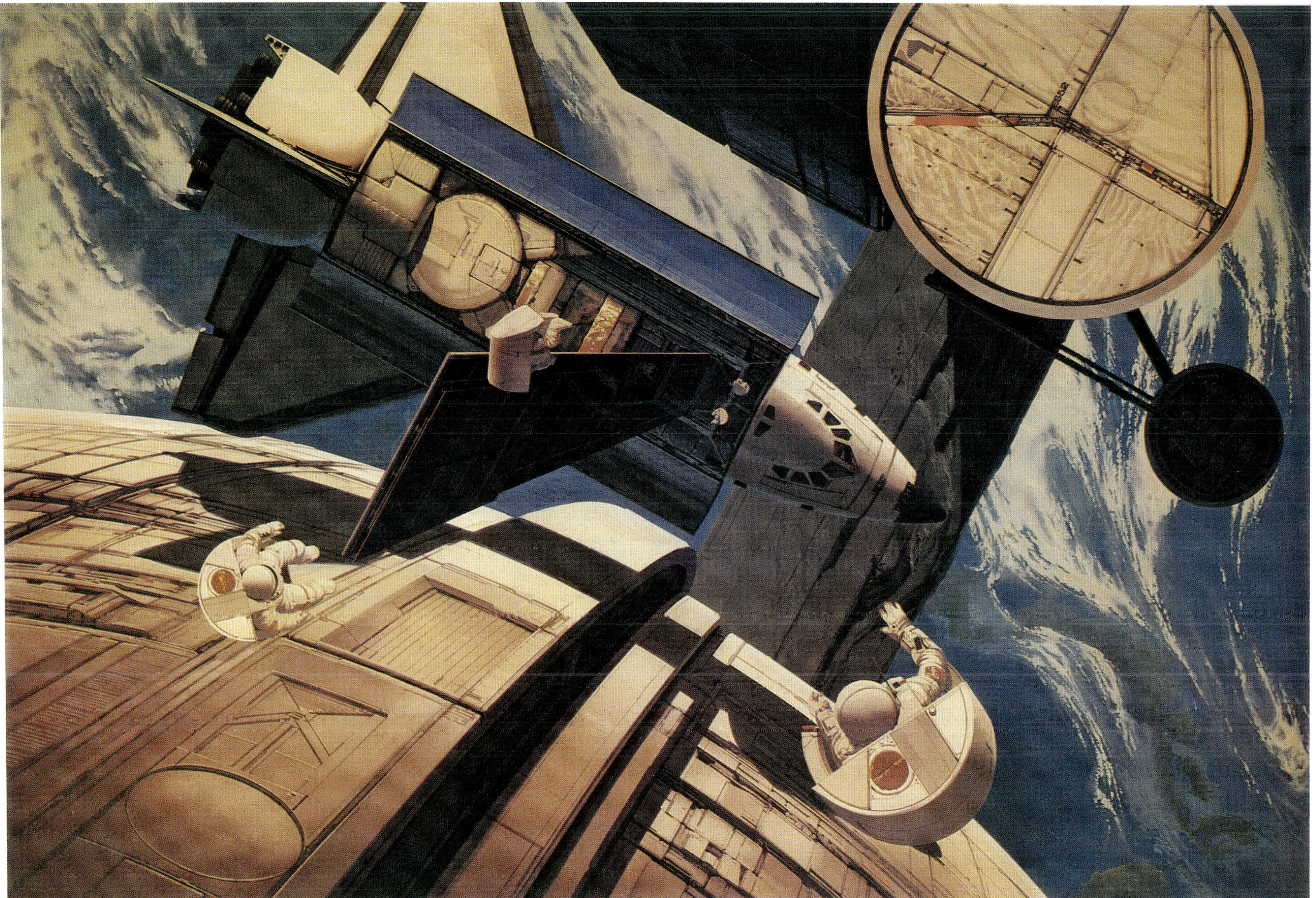

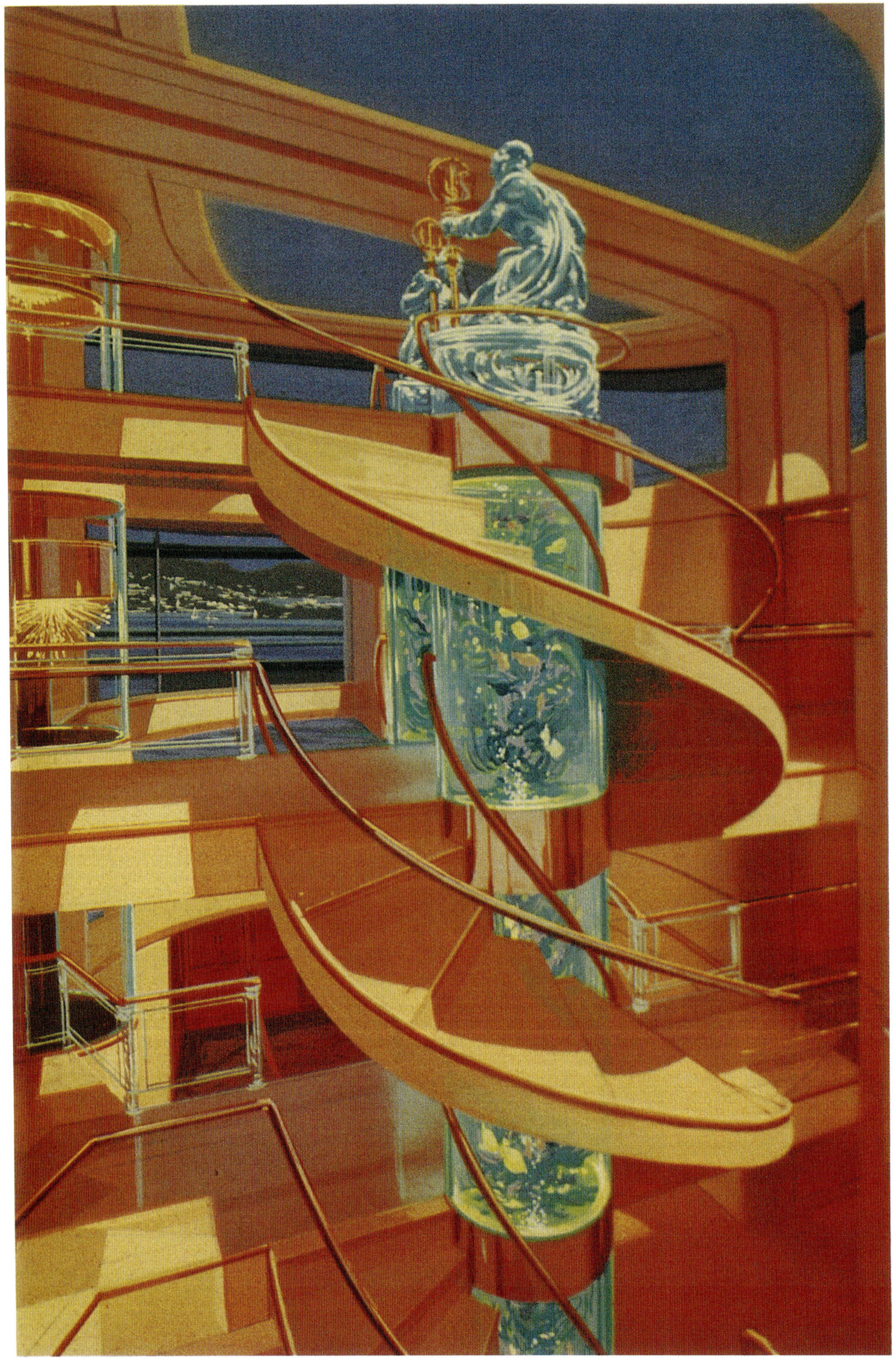

Originally published as

# "STUDIO IMAGE THREE"

Published by OBLAGON, INC.
1716 N. GARDNER ST.
LOS ANGELES, CA 90046

FAX: (213) 851-9642
PHONE: (213) 850-5225
OBLAGON REP: Roger Servick

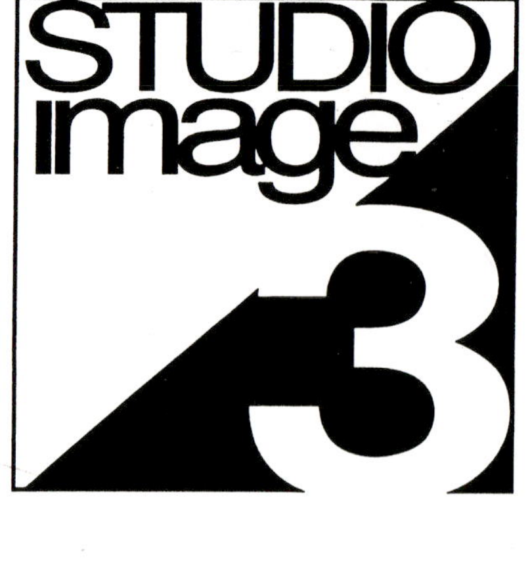


COMMISSIONING ENTITIES FOR THE FOLLOWING WORKS:

| | |
|---|---|
| 2. | PMC for CHO-SENKO |
| 5. | LANDMARK ENTERTAINMENT |
| 6. 7. | STUDIO ZOO for HONDA MOTOR CORP. |
| 8. 9. | LANDMARK ENTERTAINMENT |
| 10. 11. | LANDMARK ENTERTAINMENT |
| 12. 13. | LANDMARK ENTERTAINMENT |
| 14. 15. | COLUMBIA TELEVISION |
| 16. 17. | FOX TELEVISION |
| 18. 19. | HOLLYWOOD PICTURES |
| 20. 21. | HOLLYWOOD PICTURES |
| 22. | HOLLYWOOD PICTURES |
| 23. | NHK TV |
| 24. 25. | NHK TV |
| 26. | PETER HAYMNS PRODUCTIONS |
| 27. | DYFLEX |
| 28. | DYFLEX |
| 29. | 20TH CENTURY FOX |
| 30. 31. | 20TH CENTURY FOX |
| 32. | CORELAND  TECHNOLOGIES |
| 32. 33. | DENTSU — OSAKA |
| 34. 35. | NIPPON STEEL, LTD. |

| | |
|---|---|
| All Illustrations: | Syd Mead |
| Executive Producer: | Roger Servick |
| Layout Artist: | Ray Herron |
| Layout Design: | Syd Mead, Inc. |



Published 1994
Printed by PRINTWORKS, La Crescenta, CA

ISBN-0-929463-02-1

**Reissue by Design Studio Press**
**March, 2024**
**Printed in China, 978-1624650-80-2**